Here I Am, Lord

Lonni Collins Pratt
with Father Daniel Homan, O.S.B.

Here I Am, Lord

A Prayer Journal for Teens

Our Sunday Visitor Publishing Division
Our Sunday Visitor, Inc.
Huntington, Indiana 46750

International Standard Book Number: 0-87973-929-0
Library of Congress Catalog Card Number: 97-69272

Cover design by Tyler Ottinger

PRINTED IN THE UNITED STATES OF AMERICA

929

To my mentors and spiritual guides,
the Sylvestrine Benedictines

Acknowledgments

Excerpted from *Can You Drink the Cup?* by Henri J. M. Nouwen. Copyright © 1996 by Ave Maria Press, Notre Dame, IN 46556. Used with permission of the publisher.

Adapted from *Lessons of the Heart* by Patricia H. Livingston. Copyright © 1992 by Patricia Livingston. Used with permission of Ave Maria Press, Notre Dame, IN 46556.

Friend of the Soul: A Benedictine Spirituality of Work by Norvene Vest. Reprinted by permission. This book is available from Cowley Publications, 28 Temple Place, Boston, MA 02111 (1-800-225-1534).

From *All You Really Needed to Know About Prayer You Can Learn from the Poor* by Louise Perrotta. Copyright © 1996 by Food For The Poor. Published by Servant Publications, P.O. Box 8617, Ann Arbor, Michigan, 48107. Used with permission.

Taken from *Windows of the Soul* by Ken Gire. Copyright © 1996 by Ken Gire. Used by permission of Zondervan Publishing House.

Reprinted from *The Singer* by Calvin Miller. Copyright by InterVarsity Christian Fellowship/USA. Used by permission from InterVarsity Press, P.O. Box 1400, Downers Grove, IL 60515.

Reprinted from *Finding Happiness in the Most Unlikely Places* by Donald McCullough. Published by InterVarsity Christian Fellowship. Out of print. Used with permission from the author.

Excerpted from *Letters from the Desert* by Carlo Carretto; published and copyright © 1991 by Darton, Longman and Todd Ltd., and used by permission of the publishers.

"She Thinks I'm Real" from *Illustrations Unlimited* by Frederick B. Speakman; edited by James S. Hewitt. Copyright © 1988. Used by permission of Tyndale House Publishers, Inc. All rights reserved.

Excerpt from *Coloring Outside the Lines* by John Westfall. Copyright © 1991. Reprinted by permission of HarperCollins Publishers, Inc.

Excerpted from *The Longing for Home: Recollections and Reflections* by Frederick Buechner. Copyright © 1996 by Frederick Buechner. Reprinted by permission of HarperCollins Publishers, Inc.

Excerpted from *Dakota: A Spiritual Geography*. Copyright © 1993 by Kathleen Norris. Reprinted by permission of Ticknor and Fields/Houghton Mifflin Co. All rights reserved.

The Love of God, written and recorded by the late Rich Mullins. Copyright © 1990 BMG Songs, Inc. (ASCAP). All rights reserved. Used by permission.

Wild Heart, written by Gordon Kennedy and Randy Holland. Copyright © 1995 Ariose Music/Polygram International Publishing, Inc.; recorded for Sparrow by Phil Keaggy.

Contents

Contents Continued

Preface

Father Daniel Homan and I wrote *Here I Am, Lord* to serve two audiences. It is, first and foremost, a book to help teenagers grow in prayer. We hope they will read and study it, carry it around with them, write in it, use it. But we also had an older group of readers in mind — parents, pastors, and youth workers who love their teenage children and friends and talk to them about the important things in life. Younger and older readers will use this material in different ways. The two "notes to the reader" that follow this preface describe these differences in more detail.

First, however, who are "we"?

I started working with teenagers when I entered my own teen years, and I've never really stopped. I studied youth ministry in college, taught teens in school, worked with teens on a secular teen publication, helped design and lead youth retreats. Along the way, my husband and I have raised five children through their teen years and beyond. We have also tried to give a home to troubled and lonely teens from time to time. At an age when our peers are empty-nesters, our home is still crammed with young adults trying to make their way in this complicated world.

I also developed a particular interest in helping young people use the written word to build their spiritual lives. I am a writer and editor. I believe passionately in the power of words to lead us to the knowledge of the Word.

My collaborator is Father Daniel Homan, a Benedictine monk who has been surrounded by young people throughout his priestly ministry. Father Dan is Prior of his community, St. Benedict Monastery in Oxford, Michigan. For the last twenty-five years, Father Dan and Mary Cummings, his partner in retreat ministry, have hosted tens of thousands of teenagers in a bustling retreat house nestled on a quiet hill in Oxford. A few times, I've had the privilege of working with them.

The vast majority of these young people are members of parish youth groups or students at Catholic schools. They come from all over with their youth leaders and often their teachers and priests. During the school year, you're as likely to find teenagers at St. Benedict Monastery as you are monks.

Father Dan and I have dedicated most of our lives to loving and serving teenagers. We have worked together and we have worked with others. Many young people have touched our lives. This book flows out of our work with these wonderful young people.

The book also flows out of the Benedictine way of life. Father Dan exudes a spirit of highly contagious Benedictine spirituality, a spirit that swept me up a few years ago. St. Benedict gave us a practical, realistic way to cope with the demands of real life. He teaches us to shape the ordinary into a way to God. We learn how to handle our lives. We learn about loving and community, about reverently touching and using, about imposing some sort of order and rhythm to our lives, about the high and holy value of work and leisure. The Rule of St. Benedict contains immense wisdom that makes enormous sense in our crowded lives. It is a way long practiced by Benedictine monks and nuns, but one that speaks squarely to contemporary people.

There would be no book without Father Dan. He patiently read page upon page, helped make applications, suggested changes, gave some of his best stories and illustrations, and he encouraged me to keep writing, time after time. He insisted that we address the big, tough issues that teens face, and he defined those issues. Together we selected which stories would stay, which wouldn't. We considered titles; we listened together to the sounds of the stories and the lessons learned from them. He has spent countless hours sifting through papers side by side with me. I drew unabashedly from the deep well of his experience and wisdom.

If there is personality between the lines, it is Father Dan's and not mine. I simply watched him live and took notes. He does not want to be perceived as anything exceptional. He describes himself as "consultant" to this book. It is an inaccurate term; he is my partner and collaborator in this project. He is also my revered friend.

I am indebted to the monks of St. Benedict Monastery and the Sunday community of friends at the monastery for the lessons in community reflected here. Particularly Brother Damien and Brother Antony, who work with Father Dan and Mary on the staff of the Subiaco retreat house. Their untamed joy has often been a source of inspiration for me. Mary Cummings, who has worked faithfully beside Father Dan in youth ministry longer than anyone else, has been patient and good-natured while I invaded her space. Thank you, Mary.

I'm grateful to David and Val, who proofed pages, helped me focus, and who continue to love me well. My daughters Shelly and Andrea have long been the grist for my writing mill. They flinch every now and then but remain kind to their mother.

One last thank-you goes to Jim Manney, my editor at Our Sunday Visitor, who has handled my words with grace for many years now. Jim encouraged us to write this. He is the force behind it. Not only does he know how to make a writer sound good, he is good at friendship.

Lonni Collins Pratt

About This Book: A Note to Teens

A cynic once said: "Christians tell me that Jesus is the answer, but I want to know: What's the question?"

A clever remark. But maybe the cynic had forgotten what it was like to be young, and to have a million questions. Father Dan Homan and I have gotten to know many young people, and every one of them has had questions. Big questions. Why am I here? Who will love me? What's important and what's not? Why has this terrible thing happened to me? How shall I live my life?

We suspect that you ask questions like these too. Father Homan and I put this book together to help you wrestle with them. As you do, we think you will find answers too. Rather — an answer. The answer is not a philosophical concept, or a set of rules, or a blinding flash of mystical insight. The answer is a person — Jesus Christ. He lived in history and he's alive today. He is God's answer to human questions. The key to life, we believe, is getting into a relationship with Jesus. That's what we hope this book will help you do.

Too simple, you say? Glib? An easy religious formula for problems that hurt, that keep you awake at night?

We'll plead guilty to the charge of simplicity. Jesus is God's Word, and anyone can hear him. Men, women, and children who cannot read or write know him and love him. So do people whose minds do not work well, who suffer from the most terrible afflictions, who are starving, imprisoned, friendless, despised. They understand because Jesus is love, and every human being has a divine capacity to give and receive love. In the end, and in the beginning as well, the answer is simple.

But the fact that the answer is simple doesn't mean that it's easy. "It's not easy being green," sang Kermit the Frog. "It's not easy being a Christian," we sing back. It stands to reason that this would be so. Jesus was a human being, and it's not easy being a human being, as you well know. That means that God himself knows all your troubles and questions from the inside. He knows about failure and pain. He knows what it means to be lonely and misunderstood and rejected. He also knows the deep satisfactions of friendship, of love, of beauty and joy. Jesus is your all-knowing and all-loving companion on your journey. He is the best companion you could possibly have.

So get to know Jesus better. You get to know Jesus in the same way that you get to know any person — by spending time with him, listening to him, talking to him. That's what this book is for. Think of it as a guidebook to communicating with your traveling companion — a sort of interactive telephone-computer-television-keyboard-reference book-journal that works only when you're alone at a time of relative peace and quiet. Father Homan and I have designed it to give you several different ways to get in touch with Jesus, your best and wisest friend. Here's how we've set it up.

Each of the sessions (or chapters) starts with **Something to Think About**. This is usually a story (you'll find a couple of poems and songs in there too) that illustrates the kind of hard-to-take problem that you run into all the time. Some of these are first-person stories from our own lives. Some are stories others have told us. Some are taken from books we've read.

Think about this story. We mean it. Take some time to reflect on it. Read it twice or three times if you want. What does the story mean to you? What issue is it presenting?

The next section is called **Making It Mine**. This is a reflection or commentary or even another story that looks at the theme from another point of view. It's an invitation for you to put yourself into the scene. The first section asks you to *think*. This section asks you to exercise your *imagination*. Ask, "What if this were me…?"

Then you're invited to *pray*. The first part of the **Prayer Starter** section is a verse or two from Scripture. Most of these are quotes from the Psalms. The word "psalm" means "song." These are the ancient prayers of the Jewish people that Catholics and other Christians still pray every day. The Psalms are prayers in themselves; they are also excellent prayer "starters" — ways to begin to talk to God in a personal and sustained way.

The second part of the **Prayer Starter** section is a prayer that Father Homan and I have written. A couple are prayers associated with great Christians. These prayers are based on the theme of the day. We make no special claims for the eloquence and beauty of these prayers. They are intended to help *you* pray *your* prayer. As you pray, talk to Jesus. Talk to him about your feelings and thoughts. If you are burdened or sad or frightened or disappointed, admit your feelings to him. If you are excited or thrilled or bursting with enthusiasm, share these emotions with Jesus as well. Then listen to him. He will speak. Count on it. Jesus is love, and you can rest in his love.

The last section is called **Soul Writing**. We've given you room to do it right here in this book. We offer a suggestion for something for you to write about. Take up your pen and write. Express your feelings. Write down what the Lord said to you. Record any new insights you've had.

Writing comes easily for some people, hard for others. We encourage you to try it and stick with it even if it is difficult. Record what is happening to you. If you run short of time, jot down a few quick responses, perhaps key phrases that will jar your memory so you can write more when you have time later in the day. Just be sure to come back to it when you have more time. Write until you have nothing more to say.

Work out your pattern for going through this prayer journal. There are fifty sessions. You can do them in fifty consecutive days, five days a week for ten weeks, once a week for fifty weeks or other combinations. Some of you will be praying this book on your own. Others will be praying it with their youth group, on retreat, or with friends. If you are working through this book on your own, try to talk to someone else regularly about the issues that come up. You will find the journey is wonderfully richer when shared with a few trusted others.

Work on these prayer sessions at a time when you can be quiet inside. Some people can quiet their spirits in the middle of chaos, but most of us need a quiet place. Turn off the music. Go some place where you can be alone. Sit in a comfortable position with your back supported or lie on the floor. Take a few deep breaths, releasing each one slowly, and as each breath flows out of you, release tension and your hectic thinking patterns. You can learn to do this in just three or four minutes if you practice. Think of your body as being very heavy, as if made out of lead. Breathe deeply a few more times and when you feel quiet inside — begin reading.

You might start with the simple four-word prayer that is the title of this prayer journal: *Here I Am, Lord*. That's the main thing. The Lord is there for you too.

Lonni Collins Pratt
Father Daniel Homan, O.S.B.

About This Book: A Note to Parents, Pastors, Teachers, and Youth Ministers

Here I Am, Lord is a book for prayer. Specifically, it's aimed at helping teenagers pray. It rests on a foundation of profound respect for the spiritual lives of young people and a conviction that God is already at work in their hearts. Some doubt this. They see teenagers lost in a fog of sex, drugs, rock 'n' roll, irony, aimlessness, and materialism. But we think that an excessive emphasis on these ills, as real as they are, is itself a kind of fog. Teens, by and large, wrestle with the same issues that adults do. They flee from the pressures of their lives in basically the same ways that adults do. And they are too often misunderstood, as too often adults are as well.

One thing we've learned is that teens pray. They don't talk about it to most adults, but they admit it among themselves. They hardly let a day get by without praying. They pray about personal concerns; they pray for their families and friends and for the world. They ask God hard questions. They shudder and cry and rage for only God to see. They reflect on decisions they are making and the things they are feeling. Teenagers are fierce about praying. Their prayer is strong, gritty, practical, and idealistic. That's the kind of prayer we hope to offer in these pages.

There are many ways this book can be used. Teens can pray the book on their own, over a period of time on a daily or weekly basis. A group of young people can use this book to pray together. It could be the core of a parish youth program or a Catholic school religion class. It can be read cover to cover or just opened to a page when the moment strikes. It is intended to launch prayer, to jump-start the experience. But it doesn't channel prayer in a particular way — except to point toward the Father, Son, and Holy Spirit. The young people praying will pray in their own ways, and their experiences of prayer will be different.

The format of the book is straightforward. There are fifty prayer "sessions"; each contains four parts. **Something to Think About** offers a reading to ponder — usually a story. **Making It Mine** suggests a personal application, sometimes by presenting another story, sometimes a personal reflection. The **Prayer Starter** offers two ways into personal prayer: some Scripture, usually some verses from the Psalms, and a prayer focused on the theme of the session.

The final section of each prayer sitting is called **Soul Writing**. This section introduces questions and thoughts that are intended to move the user from reflection to action. The system used is a modified kind of *Lectio Divina*, a Benedictine tradition of reflective, prayerful reading in which we open ourselves to hearing and being present to God.

Teachers, education directors, and youth ministers will find this book jammed with stories, illustrations, and lessons that can be used in many ways in work with young people.

An entire group who work through the prayer starters and stories together will find that community is built as they talk about the big issues and share themselves with the others in the group.

Facilitators can use these stories and reflection to launch discussion and keep it lively. They can use the material for youth meetings, retreats, special events — whenever they need to prepare a lesson or talk. Fifty stories should be about right for Lent or Advent and could be incorporated into any programs designed for these times of the year also.

In order to make the book easy to use, the chapter/sessions are numbered and often include simple introductions that set the stage. Each section is short; it could be read through in about five minutes.

If you like the authors and musicians you meet in these pages, you might want to follow up by finding more of their work in book and music stores. We quote writers and musicians whose work is popular with young people. Stories and music "work" — at least in our experience with the fairly large sample of American Catholic and other Christian teenagers who've come to our retreats and workshops and summer programs.

Prayer is not as much about the words we say to God as it is about hearing God and answering God. Prayer is about a relationship, and about living side by side with God, who is closer than our own breath, the Creator who shares every moment of our lives. Prayer is the adventure of a lifetime. We hope this book will enhance that adventure for many.

Lonni Collins Pratt
Father Daniel Homan, O.S.B.

1

"Keep Running Anyway"

Something to Think About

Patti Wilson was a child when she learned she had epilepsy. One day when she was a teenager, she told her father, Jim, an avid jogger, that she wished she could jog with him but was frightened of having a seizure. Her father thought about it. His daughter's fear was reasonable, but he didn't like the idea of her being afraid. Finally he said, "Well, you might have a seizure, but if you do, I know how to handle it. You'll never be alone. Let's run."

That's what they did. Every day they ran. One day Patti said that she'd like to break the world's long-distance running record for women. The farthest any woman had run at that time was eighty miles. As a freshman in high school she determined she would run from Orange County to San Francisco, four hundred miles. As a sophomore she wanted to run fifteen hundred miles to Portland; as a junior she'd run to St. Louis, two thousand miles; and as a senior she'd run to the White House — some three thousand miles away from her Orange County home.

In her freshman year Patti completed her run to San Francisco wearing a T-shirt that read "I Love Epileptics." Her father ran every mile at her side; her mother followed in a motor home. In her sophomore year she set out for Portland. Her classmates built a huge sign that said "Run, Patti, Run" (the title of her book). But on her way to Portland she fractured a bone. The doctor said she'd have to stop running.

"You don't understand," she said. "This isn't a whim of mine, or my need to prove something. I'm doing it to break the chains on the brain that limit so many of us. Isn't there a way I can keep running?"

The doctor said he could wrap it instead of using a cast, but it would be extremely painful and would blister.

"Wrap it," she said.

She finished the Portland run, completing the last mile with Oregon's governor. After four months she completed her run to the White House where she told the President, "I wanted people to know that epileptics are normal people with normal lives." Patti admits that, above all, she needed to know she was a normal person with a normal life.

We don't have to live "under" circumstances. We can wrestle with the circumstance; we can pin it under us and make it yield the hidden good within it.

Making It Mine

Hemingway said, "Life breaks many of us and afterward we are strong at the broken places." Patti Wilson took on her worst fears for all the world to see; in doing so she gave courage and self-worth to thousands of people. Because of her own honest struggle with her personal fears, enough money has been raised to open up nineteen multimillion-dollar epileptic centers around the country. Patti didn't just become strong in the broken places, she mended the broken places of others too.

None of us are without fears. Many of those fears are based on something concrete — a physical limitation or a circumstance we can't do anything about. We don't have to live "under" circumstances. We can wrestle with the circumstance; we can pin it under us and make it yield the hidden good within it. It takes courage to push past fear and pain. It takes a normal person with a normal life. What can you do to begin tackling your own fears?

Prayer Starter

I am still confident of this:
    I will see the goodness of the Lord
    in the land of the living.
Wait for the Lord;
    be strong and take heart
    and wait for the Lord.

                                        Psalm 27:13-14

Lord Jesus, the voice of my fears sometimes shouts down all other voices. Give me courage to rise above it and believe I will see goodness and courage in the land of the living.

Soul Writing

What fears are the most intense and personal for you? How are you wrestling with these fears? How could prayer help you? What could ease your fears?

2
Choose Joy

Something to Think About

Jean-Hubert and Moise are brothers in Haiti, one of the poorest places on earth.

"When school opened this year, I couldn't go because I didn't have any shoes," says Jean-Hubert. "I knew that my mother didn't have any money to buy them for me either. But I really wanted to go to school, so I prayed that Bondye [means 'good God' in native Creole] would find me a way to get some shoes." He did, through the nuns who gave Jean-Hubert some money for his purchase.

Every night Moise kneels down in the corner of the shanty where he lives, in front of a picture of Jesus that is tacked to the wall, to pray ten Hail Marys. "I say to Bondye: My night is in your hands."

Even amidst the clatter of the cooking pots being scrubbed at high noon in the soup kitchen courtyard it's easy to picture these brothers entrusting themselves to God in the stillness of the night, here in this country [Haiti] where life seems so fragile, so vulnerable. They entrust others to his care too. A sister too sick to get up. A brother and a cousin who have died....

"If I didn't have Bondye in my life, I wouldn't have faith that things will get better," says Jean-Hubert. He is concerned about the future, of course. Would anyone look forward to hunger, or to a lifetime of standing in soup lines?

There is no way for Jean-Hubert — or anyone else, for that matter — to know what the future holds. But for this young man in the torn shirt, there is this heartening reality: he does not face it alone. "I know Bondye and he always takes care of me."

From *All You Really Need to Know About Prayer You Can Learn from the Poor* by Louise Perrotta

When an airplane pilot is in trouble he uses a code phrase for his desperate or threatening situation. He gets on the radio and says, "No joy!"

Making It Mine

When we hear about people like Moise and Jean-Hubert, an initial reaction can be guilt. Guilt for having so much. It's a rather pointless guilt, since we aren't responsible for where we are born. We do nothing to merit our comfortable lifestyles. Gratitude and joy are more appropriate responses.

On returning from Haiti, a friend who works with a well-known relief agency commented that the worst part for him was the utter despair, not the Haitians' despair but his own.

"I left thinking, 'This will never change, it can't. It's hopeless. Whatever we do, it won't be enough.' "

His own despair, however, was not matched by the way the people saw their situation. He asked people how they avoided despair and was told that they're "too busy surviving" to bother with despair. In the case of the two brothers we've met, they have made a choice against despair, even when dreams for their future seem hopeless.

They have chosen joy. Someone told me recently that when an airplane pilot is in trouble he uses a code phrase for his desperate or threatening situation. He gets on the radio and says, "No joy!"

"No joy" is the choice lots of people make. It results mostly from a lack of gratitude and the inability to see what is good in a present situation. You don't have to fool yourself to find a reason for joyful thinking and living. Every one of us has reasons for joy. A joyful attitude begins with gratitude. In prayer, give thanks for whatever situation you find yourself in. Choose Joy over No Joy.

Prayer Starter

Unless the Lord had given me help,
   I would soon have dwelt in the silence of death.
When I said, "My foot is slipping,"
   your love, O Lord, supported me.

Psalm 94:17-18

Jean-Hubert's prayer: "Good Father, Bondye, my life is in your hands. Open the door of heaven to provide what I need today. Even before my prayer is on my lips you know what it will be — for shoes ... a decent job ... protection ... help for those I love ... hope for the future. Take care of me again today and keep me very close to you, so that one day I may see you open the door of heaven and welcome me home."

 # Soul Writing

Write down something you are grateful for. Something that gives you joy right now. Now, read Jean-Hubert's prayer again. Notice how similar it is to the Our Father, the prayer Jesus taught us. Make up your own prayer as Jean-Hubert did, a prayer of love and thanks and gratitude.

3
"My Father Can See Me Play"

Something to Think About

Lou Little was the football coach at Columbia University years ago. Lou recalls the day a boy tried out for the football team who wasn't very good. However, the boy had a certain determination of spirit and contagious enthusiasm. Lou thought he'd be good for the team.

"He'll never be able to play," Lou told someone, "but at least he'll be on the bench encouraging the others."

The coach gradually came to admire and care for that young man. He would often see him around campus walking with his father, leading his father in fact, because his father was obviously blind. The boy was never ashamed of his father; they talked and laughed as if they hardly knew anyone was watching. Other times they walked together silently close.

Then one day Lou got a call informing him the boy's father had died.

A week or so later, the young man returned to campus, just before the big game of the year. Lou went to him and asked, "Can I do anything for you? Can I help? Just name it, son, anything at all." To the coach's astonishment he replied, "I want to start in the game." Lou was stunned. The boy had never asked to play before, but a promise was a promise. The coach started him.

Imagine everyone's surprise when on the first play from scrimmage, this young man single-handedly made a tackle that threw the opposing team for a loss. He went on to play as if he had fire in his bones. He was so exceptional that Lou left him in for the whole game.

When the game was over, Coach Little and other players asked him, "What happened out there today?" The boy grinned, "Today was the first time my Dad ever got to see me play!"

Faith inspires

his greatness.

Faith can fuel

us to play above

our heads and

believe Someone

is watching

and cheering.

Making It Mine

We all dream of excelling, of playing in the game with a courage and fire that exceeds any reasonable expectation. We get stuck in mediocrity or have to live with very real imposed limits, yet we can know moments when something like divine fire takes hold of us. In that instant, we are more than we ever dreamed of being. Maybe if we could catch whatever it is that calls the fire down, we could live above mediocrity more often.

In our story, the young man's passion is ignited by the love of his father. He believes with everything he has, including his talent, mind, and body, that his father is more alive than ever, with clear vision at last, cheering in the stands someplace. Faith fuels his passion. Faith inspires his greatness. Faith can fuel us to play above our heads and believe Someone is watching and cheering.

 ## Prayer Starter

For God will command his angels concerning you
   to guard you in all your ways;
they will lift you up in their hands,
   so that you will not strike your foot against a stone.
You will tread upon the lion and the cobra;
   you will trample the great lion and the serpent.

                     Psalm 91:11-13

Father, I don't always feel as if someone's cheering for me or watching over me in the game of life. There's a loneliness in me I can hardly speak of. Give me faith. I want to believe I'm not totally alone in this game.

Soul Writing

Imagine you are standing in the middle of a football field in an empty stadium. Slowly, one by one, imagine the stands filling up with people who have encouraged you, loved you, been a friend when you needed one. Imagine God in the stands. Write about the people and what they mean to you.

4
Agnes Hears God

Something to Think About

Agnes Bojaxhiu went to India to be a missionary. For eighteen years she was a nun at St. Mary's High School in Calcutta, a comfortable, clean convent, where she worked teaching upper-class girls and enjoying her work.

On August 16, 1948, she left the convent. She remembers closing the door and having a fear and dread grip her such as she had never felt before.

"Leaving the Congregation of Our Lady of Loreto was the biggest sacrifice of my life," she said. "I suffered a lot when I was eighteen, and left my family and country to go to the convent. But I suffered a lot more when I left the convent to begin the new experience that Jesus had proposed."

Without her religious habit, she shut the door behind her and walked out, owning nothing. She had received permission to start a new order, but there was no one but her, alone in Calcutta. She clutched hard to her conviction that God had called her to begin a new life.

This woman did a courageous thing — an expression of total love and faith. And from it a miracle happened: the world was given the extraordinary life and love of Agnes Bojaxhiu, later to be known as Mother Teresa. (She died on September 5, 1997.)

She spent months living like the poor. She was one of them now — with no home, no savings, no work, and no family. She ate rice and salt as they did. She took nursing courses from Mother Dengal and her Medical Missionary Sisters in Patna and after a few months she returned to Calcutta. She returned to the slum located right behind St. Mary's High School — in the shadow of her former comfortable life. While she was living at the convent she had never wanted to even get near the slum. Now it was her home. A week after setting herself up in a tiny shack she began teaching again. She had once taught the daughters of rich families only a few steps away. Now, in the suffocating heat of her shack, with sweat and filth invading her body, she began teaching children no one cared about — "the children of nobodies," she says. A week after moving into the shack she had twenty-five children.

In the suffocating heat of her shack, with sweat and filth invading her body, she began teaching children no one cared about — "the children of nobodies," she says. A week after moving into the shack she had twenty-five children.

Agnes soon penetrated deep into the misery of Calcutta's poorest to discover atrocious, unbelievable suffering. Before long a few women joined her and one by one a community formed. Before Mother Teresa passed away, her every word made headlines, and her name continues to be a household word; she is still one of the most admired women in the world. God sent her not to just the poor of Calcutta but to all of us. It began the day a nervous young woman closed the door on one life and walked into the mystery of the future.

Making It Mine

We call them hunches or maybe intuition. We recognize the impulse as some voice that speaks in interior regions we hardly ever visit. Responding, we call a friend or send a note. We make a decision about our future. We say something we usually wouldn't because it seems like the right thing.

It's not easy to become quiet enough to hear this voice. There's too much noise around us. It takes time to sort through what our own voice is and what it isn't. We're constantly deciding which voices are worth our time and which aren't. Slowly, if we take risks and act on the prodding of the voice, we discover it can be trusted. We come to know that "something speaks in the pine" as George MacDonald wrote. By attentive listening Mother Teresa learned to recognize the sound of God's voice. Its distinctive quality becomes as familiar as a friend's face.

Author Robert Benson remembers talking to a little girl about prayer. The child was five. Benson asked, "What does God say about you? What's he think of you?" He said the girl looked at him as if he were daft and replied, "God likes me; God likes me very much."

"How do you know that?"

"I can tell by the way he talks to me. I hear it in his voice." God's voice is the sound of a friend who likes us. Maybe that's why Mother Teresa could shut the door and walk away into whatever the future held. We trust our friends.

 # Prayer Starter

Come, let us bow down in worship,
   let us kneel before the Lord our Maker;
for he is our God
   and we are the people of his pasture,
   the flock under his care.
Today, if you hear his voice,
   do not harden your hearts....

Psalm 95:6-8a

O Lord God,
I have no idea where I am going,
I do not see the road ahead of me,
I cannot know for certain where it will end.

Nor do I really know myself,
and the fact that I think
I am following Your will
does not mean that I am actually doing so.
But I believe
that the desire to please You
does in fact please You.
And I hope I have that desire
in all that I am doing.

— Thomas Merton

Soul Writing

Think about the times something seemed to speak to your life. Maybe you followed a hunch or felt compelled to call someone and it turned out to be just the right thing. Do you think that you hear God speaking to you now about something? What might it be?

5
What We Need from the Poor

Something to Think About

It was a typical day at the soup kitchen where I cooked. I stayed in the kitchen filling plates. Every now and then I would smile at one of our guests if he or she caught my eye. It was simply the easy thing to do, and I'm shy.

My safe isolation in the kitchen was suddenly interrupted by a junior-high girl who shifted from one foot to the other and looked nervous, "Uh … there's this mess … under a table where there's like more kids than I've ever seen in my whole life…. Someone barfed up the scalloped potatoes…."

There are people who always follow up someone's vomiting with their own encore; they can't help it — it's just how their digestive system is made. At closer inspection the girl looked a little greenish.

Handing her the serving spoon, I said, "Just stand here and fill plates. You aren't going to throw up, are you?"

"No, ma'am, not if I don't have to go out there."

I went out there instead.

The mess was under a table where a young woman and five children were seated. The oldest appeared to be seven or eight. The children's mother had herded them to the end of the table away from the mess and looked embarrassed.

"I'm so sorry. Max has the flu. I just hoped he'd be able to hold something down. I guess he should have gone without dinner."

"It's no problem," I said. But it was. I didn't like being out of the kitchen. It bothered me even more than filling towel after towel with the wet mess on the floor. "What am I doing here?" I muttered under my breath.

Suddenly, a small tennis shoe lodged itself against my forehead — firmly. A young voice said, "Lady, my shoe is untied."

Grasping the foot solidly and lowering it to my lap I looked up into the eyes of a boy about four. I tied it silently keeping a strong grip on the shoe.

"This one," he said and plopped the other down. "Lady, can you talk? My name is Max. Who are you?"

Max. The culprit.

Among bandages, starving children, men and women ravaged by leprosy, poverty she had never even imagined … the girl raised like a princess found her "call" and herself. She said she found freedom. It was the gift of the poor to her.

He leaned down and put his face close to mine and said again, slowly, with careful four-year-old articulation, "My … name … is … Max. Who … are … you?"

I looked into Max's eyes then. Red-rimmed eyes, a little puffy. Runny nose. Very pale. Too thin. A lump formed in my throat. My capacity for indifference and selfishness made his question "Who are you?" poignant. Indeed, I wondered, gazing up at the pale child, who am I that this child is so easily dismissed by me?

Safe in the kitchen, there had been no pale toddlers, babies putting potatoes up their noses, or old men who smelled of urine and tobacco. At a nearby table, two elderly women packaged up half their meals to take to a young man who wasn't at the soup kitchen for dinner because he was home sick. A child recited multiplication tables to her parents. A young man told an old man about working eleven hours a day six days a week for minimum wage because his head injury had impaired his memory and he'd dropped out of college.

Suddenly, the people around the tables weren't "the poor" or "the needy" or the other "them" who were the object of my benevolence. They went from being nameless objects to being people in the short time it took me to finish tying Max's other shoe.

 ## Making It Mine

Marion Preminger was born in a castle in Hungary to a wealthy royal family, surrounded by maids, nannies, and chauffeurs. When she was eighteen, she married a handsome young man, the son of a wealthy family. The marriage lasted a year. She began a career as an actress and met Otto Preminger, German director. They married. They moved to America, where his career took off. Marion got caught up in the fast lane and started moving from man to man. Preminger divorced her. She moved to Paris.

In 1948 she read about the work of Dr. Albert Schweitzer in Africa. Something stirred inside her.

She found Schweitzer playing the organ in a village church in France where he was visiting. He invited her to dinner. Marion said she had "found what I've been looking for all my life." She became a disciple of sorts, eventually moving to Africa to work in a hospital with Schweitzer.

Among bandages, starving children, men and women ravaged by leprosy, poverty she had never even imagined … the girl raised like a princess found her "call" and herself. She said she found freedom. It was the gift of the poor to her.

Often, we view our chances to serve the needy as if we are doing someone a favor. Marion Preminger claimed that the poorest of the poor in Africa gave her back herself. In a profound way, we find ourselves when we look in the eyes of the poor and face the question "Who are you?" It's the poor who do us a favor by accepting the feeble attempts at benevolence we make so halfheartedly. Those who have made a life of service to the poor would argue that they who are perceived as *givers* are actually *receivers*.

Prayer Starter

You know my folly, O God;
  my guilt is not hidden from you.
The poor will see and be glad —
  you who seek God, may your hearts live!
The Lord hears the needy
  and does not despise his captive people.

Psalm 69:5, 32-33

God of the poor, I find it easy to feel sorry for the poor in general, but I don't want to have much to do with real poor people. I need poor people in my life. Help me see this. Show me how to serve the poor with real compassion and understanding.

Soul Writing

Write about poor people and your attitude toward them.

"When I see pictures of the very poor or the homeless on the street I feel_____."

6
Kissing Twisted Lips

Something to Think About

Richard Selzer, M.D., in his book Mortal Lessons, *tells the story of a young woman who has undergone surgery that severed a nerve connected to a facial muscle.*

Following surgery, the young woman's mouth had what the author described as a clownish twist. Surgery had been necessary to remove a tumor from her face.

Selzer watches as the youthful husband of the woman tries to assure her that all will be well. What is changed, what is missing, will not make any difference in their life and their love. Even though she has been told that her mouth will always be a bit crooked because of the surgery.

Without a blink upon hearing of his wife's permanent little twist, the young man leans down and kisses her.

"I can see how he twists his own lips to accommodate hers, to show her that their kiss still works," the author writes.

Making It Mine

In the movie *Labyrinth* a young girl is on a mission to save her baby brother from the evil gnome of a king. It's a tough journey. At every turn she collides with another obstacle. However, she also makes friends and finds companions to share the ups and downs of the adventure.

The most dreaded and worst obstacle is the Bog of Eternal Stench. Doesn't make you want to go there, does it? This giant puddle of slime not only smells beyond description, it comes complete with a curse: Get any of that slimy crud on your person and it stays forever and ever.

Our weary pilgrims have a little problem crossing the foul lake of stinking slime. They are trapped in the middle of the thing, standing on the only safe ground. Then the ground beneath their shivering toes begins to sink. There is no hope. There is no way out. They are destined for permanent "stinkiness."

At the very darkest edge-of-your-seat moment one of the girl's companions (a gentle monster sort) throws back his head and lets out an earsplitting howl. Suddenly, the ooze churns and bubbles and rolls.

God isn't hesitant about kissing twisted lips or getting us out of stinkiness. God is our friend.

A rock rises out of the foul pit. The whole frightened little group gets on the rescuing rock and glides out of danger.

Safe on nonstinky solid land, the little girl turns to the creature who had wailed and asks why the rock did that — and how did he know the rock would do it?

The hairy thing answers with simple and wise sense, "Rock … my friend."

Both stories are good theology. Life misshapes us. It also puts us in some treacherous places. God isn't hesitant about kissing twisted lips or getting us out of stinkiness. God is our friend. God likes us. When we least expect it, there's a kiss of assurance or a friend who sees us safely home.

 # Prayer Starter

Why are you downcast, O my soul?
   Why so disturbed within me?
Put your hope in God,
   for I will yet praise him,
   my Savior and my God.
By day the Lord directs his love,
   at night his song is with me —
   a prayer to the God of my life.

Psalm 42:5, 8

Assurance and safety are hard to come by, Father. Give me courage to believe you really do care about me and will be with me whatever happens.

Soul Writing

Imagine that God is talking to one of the angels about you. What would God say? Write it down.

7
Drinking from the Outcast's Cup

Something to Think About

Before his death in 1996, Father Henri Nouwen worked with disabled persons in the Daybreak community in Toronto. Trevor, born with a mental handicap, was one of those residents, and the time came when he had to be hospitalized away from Daybreak. Nouwen, who had lived at Daybreak with Trevor, decided to visit him in the hospital. They were friends. The hospital chaplain took the opportunity to invite Nouwen, a renowned author and speaker, to have lunch with a small group of hospital staff.

When I arrived … a large group of clergy and hospital personnel was waiting for me and … welcomed me warmly. I looked around for Trevor, but he wasn't there. So I said: "I came here to visit Trevor. Can you tell me where I can find him?" The hospital chaplain said: "You can be with him after lunch." I was stunned and said, "But didn't you invite him for lunch?" "No, no," he said, "that's impossible. Staff and patients cannot have lunch together. Moreover, we have reserved the Golden Room for this occasion, and no patient has ever been allowed in that room. It is for staff only."

"Well," I said, "I will have lunch with you all when Trevor can be there too. Trevor and I are close friends. It is for him I came, and I am sure he would love to join us for lunch."

I noticed some mixed reactions to my words…. I found Trevor on the hospital grounds, as always, looking for flowers. When he saw me his face lit up, and he ran up to me as if we had never been apart and said, "Henri, here are some flowers for you." Together we went to the Golden Room….

[Trevor asks for Coke, Nouwen gets a glass of wine and they sit at the table. They join the others and Nouwen is soon making small talk with someone when Trevor suddenly stood up.]

… [Trevor] stood up, took his glass of Coke, lifted it, and said with a loud voice and big smile, "Ladies and gentlemen … a toast!" Everyone dropped their conversation and turned to Trevor with puzzled and somewhat anxious faces. I could read their thoughts: "What in the heck is this patient going to do? Better be careful."

But Trevor had no worries. He looked at everybody and said: "Lift up your glasses." Everyone obeyed. And then as if it were the most

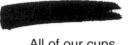

All of our cups together have emptied into the one Jesus took in his hands the night before his death, the cup he lifted and blessed. A cup of blessing.

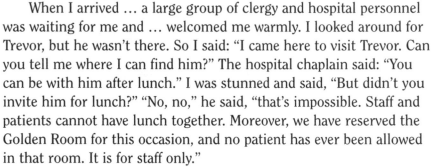

obvious thing to do, he started to sing: "When you're happy and you know it … lift your glass. When you're happy and you know it … lift your glass. When you're happy and you know it, When you're happy and you know it, When you're happy and you know it, lift your glass."

As he sang, people's faces relaxed and [everyone] started to smile. Soon a few joined Trevor in his song, and not long after, everyone was standing, singing loudly under Trevor's direction.

From *Can You Drink the Cup?* by Henri Nouwen

 # Making It Mine

The title of Henri Nouwen's book is *Can You Drink the Cup?* "The cup" is a symbol for the whole of our lives. Life is a cup God gives us to drink. Many people believe that God has given them only poison and sludge to drink in the cup. Bitter. Hard to swallow. Loss. Handicap. Misfortune. Everyone's cup is a little different.

Often, it seems to us we were handed a less-than-desirable cup to swallow. If anyone ever had a right to feel that way it's Trevor, and the Trevors of the world who are, by birth, different from the rest of us. This is what God has placed in the hands of Trevor to drink.

All of our cups together have emptied into the one Jesus took in his hands the night before his death, the cup he lifted and blessed. A cup of blessing. The cup that later that same night he shuddered to hold and still managed to offer to God. Not my cup, God, but yours. St. Paul said the cup we share is a "blessing cup."

Trevor's blessing cup still means he's dreadfully handicapped and misunderstood, even rejected by those entrusted to care for him, as in the story Nouwen tells. Your blessing cup probably seems to be a mixed cup too. That's true for all of us. What turns the mixed cup into a blessing cup?

Trevor has the idea. You lift it up, like Jesus did. You lift it and you offer it. Prayer is one way we lift our cup; loving is another. Living peacefully and quietly with hardship and trying to make the best of whatever we can't change … and then, no matter who's looking or what they're saying or thinking, we sing:

"If you're happy and you know it …"

"This is my Body. This is my Blood …"

"If you're happy and you know it …"

The cup is a toast to life. You can't lift it until you know you're happy, and you know that it's going to all work out somehow. People of faith are in on the secret of what makes humans ultimately happy. It's all in the attitude.

Whatever we might think about the content of the cup, the cup is God's gift to us. It is all we really have to offer each other, the universe … God. If you're happy and you know it … despite how bad it might look … lift your cup.

Prayer Starter

Shout for joy to the Lord, all the earth.
  Worship the Lord with gladness;
  come before him with joyful songs.
Know that the Lord is God.
  It is he who made us, and we are his;
  we are his people, the sheep of his pasture.

Psalm 100:1-3

Father, I'm not always sure the cup is filled with blessing or with anything that's good. Sometimes I see just the bitter parts. Give me the eyes to see the good in my cup. Give me the eyes of faith.

Soul Writing

Recall a situation when your positive attitude helped ease conflict or gave you or others a better perspective. Write about it. Or write about the person you know who has the most positive attitude. What is this person like?

8
Nice Things in Secret Places

Something to Think About

If you ask I'll step down to my basement office and pull out my file marked "Poetry" and bring it to you. Better still, if you ask I'll bring it upstairs and read some of the poems aloud for you — not all of them, for there are more than eight hundred in my folder. I will read the poem about my father's barn and the one about the shooting stars. I'll read the poem I wrote about the boy who wandered around in an abandoned house, or about the old woman in the nursing home who did not even remember the names of her children. There is a poem about an old woman who is speaking to her husband who has just died, which I think you would like. I would like to read to you the poem about my neighbor's porch light.

Do you have something kept in a folder that you consider to be part of yourself as is your hair or voice? We think that we are known by the names we take, by the street addresses we have, by the places we work. But I believe there are things under our beds, in the closet, tucked deep inside a drawer or in the attic, that reveal more about who we are than all the rest…. Who we are is revealed by the secrets we keep.

From *Only the Heart Knows How to Find Them*
by Christopher DeVinck

Char never told anyone back home about the boy. Maybe it's because her uncle has cerebral palsy. She had never told anyone that either.

Making It Mine

Char was fifteen when she went on a mission trip with the church youth group. She was one of those girls everyone liked — friendly, fun to be around, pretty. She was also popular, which at the time was a really important thing in her life.

The youth group made a trip to a children's hospital, bringing coloring books to the children and playing games with them. In the ward there was a six-year-old boy afflicted severely with cerebral palsy. He was tied into his wheelchair and unable to control the jerky movements of his body. He couldn't keep saliva from drooling down his bottom lip to his clothing. His head seemed permanently bent at a right angle.

The teens were told to go into that ward and pick out a child to play with. One adult remembered standing in the door of the ward watching the teens pick out children and carefully avoiding the boy in the wheelchair. She described what Char did.

In long, purposeful steps Char went straight to the boy, as if he were naturally her first choice. She squatted beside him and looked him eye to eye and said, "I don't have anyone to play with; would you help me out?"

For the next two hours they talked, colored, laughed, went for a walk in the sunshine, and watched cartoons together. Char would take the hem of her T-shirt and wipe off his chin every now and then.

The strange thing is, Char never told anyone back home about the boy. Maybe it's because her uncle has cerebral palsy. She had never told anyone that either. Maybe it's because she was still playing the popularity game. I know people who are forty-something and still do it. Maybe it was just the natural thing for her to do and so she didn't make any big deal out of it.

Char's mother heard about it from a youth chaperone and said that she felt "… a door had been opened into my daughter's soul. What I know is that no matter what happens in her life, the people who know this about Char realize who she really is." Her secret told us.

Prayer Starter

O Lord, you have searched me
   and you know me.
You know when I sit and when I rise;
   you perceive my thoughts from afar.
You discern my going out and my lying down;
   you are familiar with all my ways.
Before a word is on my tongue
   you know it completely, O Lord.

Psalm 139:1-4

God, I don't want to be ashamed of who I am. Bring to my mind the good things that I keep inside. Thank you, Father, for these bright lights in my life.

Soul Writing

If your secrets were all revealed today, what would they tell others about you? Write about "good secrets" — acts of kindness, tender feelings, a desire for what is right. Is this difficult? Why?

9
If They Opened You Up, What Would Be Inside?

Something to Think About

There's a story about Christmas in a small town in nineteenth-century England. The village has a traditional party where gifts are given to all the children. It's a highlight of the year for the village. The evening is warmed with the smiles of children. Like the Christmas parties we all recall, a tall tree glowing with light and sparkle and surrounded by festively wrapped packages welcomes the guests and beckons the youngsters eager to unwrap packages.

A young retarded man is among the villagers. He's long been the object of cruel jokes and misunderstanding. It's a miracle he even shows up.

The pile of gifts beneath the tree grows smaller and his face seems to drop with every present that is passed by him. His childlike heart hurts as everyone, except him, receives a gift. He's too old to be included with the children — but he doesn't know or understand that. Then some of the boys come to him. With suspicious grins and glances between themselves they extend a gift to him. The last one under the tree.

His face lights up. A smile breaks the corners of his mouth as he eagerly tears off the ribbons and wrappings. But as his fingers open the box, his heart breaks, confusion and pain clouding his face. The box is empty.

The packaging didn't give away the secret. The ribbons and wrapping were bright and festive. The outside didn't give any clue that the inside held only disappointment. Despite how promising the package looked, the box was empty.

It's happened to most us of us, hasn't it?

Buzz was sacked hard on the first play. And he didn't get up. He didn't get up for a very long time. I held his mother's hand while his father paled.

Then we saw him move. He sat up but didn't move his legs. One leg moved. The other didn't.

Making It Mine

Buzz was a brilliant football star in my hometown. Like fire falling from heaven. His movements almost magical. Buzz was destined to be the celebrity quarterback from a small town. In a small town, stars get lots of attention and usually end up blinded by their own sparkle. Not Buzz. He paid attention to the kids no one else ever noticed. He said nice things to other people — every single day, and he'd been doing it for as long as I had known him. He didn't have to try to be nice. It came naturally.

His smile was always ready. When you needed a hand to hold, or a shoulder to lean on, you could count on those wide shoulders and strong hands. Buzz was an all-around nice guy — and my best friend. The fuss local and state newspapers made about his future never meant much to him. He loved football, but it wasn't his life. He would run his Dad's hardware store someday, marry a local girl, be buried out of the same little parish where both of us had been baptized, confirmed, and schooled. It would be a good life, he'd say, and then smile a Buzz sort of smile that lifted one corner of his mouth and ended in a wink.

In our senior year, Buzz got a deal from a big school other boys would have died for. And he got all those little extras no one ever admitted boys like Buzz got from colleges. All wrapped up in promises, shining lights, marching bands. He was on his way up, headed for the big time. Buzz never changed, not really, not inside. But he started thinking about his future in terms of the promises and spotlight and sports cars. Words like "pro" and "Super Bowl" crept into our conversations. It was a bright dream — no one could blame him for riding it out of our small town as far as the dream would take him.

I was with his parents, along with a few other close friends from high school, the day Buzz started as quarterback in a televised game between long-standing rivals. This was the *big* game. It was Buzz's debut on national TV. The world was at his door.

Buzz was sacked hard on the first play. And he didn't get up. He didn't get up for a very long time. I held his mother's hand while his father paled. Then we saw him move. He sat up but didn't move his legs. One leg moved. The other didn't. Cameras zoomed in. Buzz glanced up. I saw one corner of his mouth lift in a painful smile, and a wink crinkled his all-American boy-next-door face. It was over, but we cheered anyway.

Buzz fractured his ankle. He never came back all the way. He finished college with honors and returned home. He was a tall, tired, Midwestern kid with a limp and a cowlick. The people who had built shrines to his athletic ability wouldn't return his phone calls.

The package, for all its trimming and ribbons and glitter, was empty. The dream came to a sudden, irreversible end. The marching band stormed off the field, and Buzz wasn't a star anymore.

Today he runs the hardware store with his ready smile, and he's still hugging people and grinning when the bottom falls out of his world, which it has a time or two.

He said later that he did get caught up in the hype for awhile, but sometime during his freshman year he realized, "… it just didn't amount to anything that really mattered. The promises were empty, the stories were lies spun for a small-town boy they thought didn't have a brain in his head."

He said he always knew that the people who loved him, the ones who mattered, were not the people pumping him with stories of fame and fortune. They were his parents and family, his lifelong friends … the people at home.

He limped home where we still considered him a hero, not because of his football pizzazz, but because he wasn't a package glittering on the outside and empty inside. Buzz is a real human being who learned early and learned well how to live and love.

You can crush the ankle of a guy like that, and he'll walk. You can toss him off a football field, and he'll stay in the game of life with a grin. The package isn't empty, and he's the real thing.

Prayer Starter

You have made my days a mere handbreadth;
    the span of my years is nothing before you.
    Each man's life is but a breath.
Man is a mere phantom as he goes to and fro:
    He bustles about, but only in vain;
    he heaps up wealth, not knowing who will get it.
"But now, Lord, what do I look for?
    My hope is in you…"

Psalm 39:5-7

Father, what is important and what isn't? Sometimes I get confused. I chase after empty dreams and pointless glitz. The ribbons and wrappings and shine keep me from looking deeper sometimes. Teach me to look deeper.

Soul Writing

Ever been there? Has a dream died for you? A promise broken? Write about how you felt when you've "been there." What did you learn? What would you do different?

10
The Saint of Auschwitz

Something to Think About

There are places you would never expect to find goodness shining, places like one of Hitler's death camps — Auschwitz. Four million people, mostly Jews, died there in World War II. If you go today you can walk in the showers that drenched them in poison gas or see the half-ton of human hair still preserved.

But there's another kind of monument that has come out of Auschwitz; it's a monument to humanity at its best — the life and memory of Maximilian Kolbe as remembered by Francis Gajowniczek, a sergeant in the Polish army. Both men were prisoners there.

Kolbe was a Franciscan priest. The Nazi atrocities did not deter Kolbe from doing small things that shone the light of Jesus in a place where you'd never expect to find it. He gave up his bunk and shared his food and said kind words. He prayed for the Nazis. Before long he was tagged "Saint of Auschwitz."

When a prisoner escaped from Auschwitz, ten prisoners were killed for the one who got away.

The commandant had the whole camp herded into the courtyard and randomly selected ten people to die. They would be put into isolation where they received no food or water until they died.

In July of Kolbe's incarceration an escape took place, and the commandant began calling names. Gajowniczek is the last named. He begins to cry, "My wife ... my children." There's something going on in the ranks of the prisoners, and the guards poise to fire their rifles. Prisoners don't talk. They don't cry. They don't move. Everyone knows it.

It's Kolbe. He's broken rank and is moving toward the commandant. That quiet calm on his face is familiar to everyone, but it's still pretty startling in a place like this. He's told to stop or be shot.

"I want to talk to the commander," he says. No fear. They don't kill him. He keeps walking and stops in front of the commandant. He makes an outrageous request. "I want to die in place of this man," he says, pointing to the sobbing Gajowniczek. "I'm old. I have no wife or children. He'll be of more use to you...." It's a logic Nazis will understand. People are commodities.

"Who are you?"

"A Catholic priest."

What is evident is Kolbe's determination to bring life to a place of death. No situation is so horrible that it crushes love completely. Whatever happens, we can find a light shining in the darkest night.

After a short, stupefied silence Kolbe's request is indifferently granted.

Gajowniczek says, "I could only thank him with my eyes. I was stunned and could hardly grasp what was going on. The immensity of it: I, the condemned, am to live and someone else willingly and voluntarily offers his life for me — a stranger. Is this some dream?"

The Saint of Auschwitz was hard to kill. He didn't die on the same timetable as the other nine. On August 14, 1941, the camp doctor injected phenol into his heart and he died. The light even Auschwitz couldn't extinguish was already burning in the man whose life Kolbe had saved — and who eventually told the world the remarkable story of Father Maximilian Kolbe. Pope John Paul II named the martyr a saint in 1982.

Making It Mine

The life of St. Maximilian Kolbe is an example of what courage, grace, and selflessness look like in the darkest of times. What is evident is the saint's determination to bring life to a place of death. No situation is so horrible that it crushes love completely. Whatever happens, we can find a light shining in the darkest night. We can be the light shining in the dark place. When our center is God, that center can stay strong whatever is happening around us.

When my teenaged daughter was in an Intensive Care Unit after a near-fatal auto accident, every breath she took was a struggle for her. Hospitals are places that wrestle with death; they are built for this reason. It was death that hung over my daughter's bed, death that seemed to be nipping at her heels. As her mother, I could do nothing but watch her slip deeper into a coma.

I'll never forget the day I walked into the ICU to find a young nurse braiding my daughter's hair. It was a senseless thing, a *beautiful* thing. That nurse had found a simple way to shine light into a very dark time. Her act said she believed this patient was going to wake up and care about how she looked, as any seventeen-year-old girl would. My child wasn't a nameless patient on the edge of becoming a mortality statistic; she was a person — someone's daughter, someone's best friend, someone's sister.

Braiding the hair of a comatized girl, I believe, was a loving act done in the same spirit that moved the Saint of Auschwitz to sacrifice his life for a fellow human being. It is an act that refuses to give death the last word, refuses to stop being human and loving in a place of death, refuses to be made ugly by the darkness. An ordinary human being is capable of extraordinary things even in Auschwitz, or, an Intensive Care Unit.

Prayer Starter

You will not fear the terror of night,
    nor the arrow that flies by day,
nor the pestilence that stalks in the darkness,
    nor the plague that destroys at midday.

Psalm 91:5-6

Heavenly Father, in the darkest times I receive once more from you this gift of light and life. Hold me in the night that I may hold myself against all that would make me what I am not. Help me see the slender wisp of a veil that keeps light from pushing back the night.

 **Soul Writing**

Write about someone you know who brought light and goodness to a terrible situation as Maximilian Kolbe did. Think of simple ways you could do the same.

11
A Cartwheel?
At a Time Like This?

Something to Think About

In the book *Learning to Say Good-bye,* author Eda LeShan tells about visiting a friend who had lost her husband. It had been one of the darkest times of this woman's life. One afternoon, they went together to the cemetery and stood at the grave talking about his life, recalling favorite memories. The widow's young children were also present.

After talking about things he'd said, things he'd dreamed for, they fell silent. Sometimes people run out of words. And, sometimes, a moment grabs us so fiercely that words can't express it.

The youngest daughter in the family, a little girl named Liz, suddenly broke from the silent huddled group, ran out to the grave, and did a cartwheel over it. LeShan was stunned. Then the girl's mother turned to her with a wide smile and said, "She hasn't done any cartwheels since her Dad died. He used to love it when she did cartwheels."

What did the little girl mean to say to her father? LeShan says, "… I realized that her gift to him was to pick up the threads of her life and to begin to live as fully as she could. The time comes to begin to do cartwheels again — to express our joy in being alive."

Can cartwheels be an Easter symbol? Why not? Some might consider it disrespectful, but they'd be wrong. That cartwheel was an offering of her life — a promise sealed in love that, because of love, life will go on. It was the child's way of saying she believed the grave wasn't the final word. She would live despite this — fully and joyfully with heels kicked up and her face lifted to the warming sun.

The Easter story is God's cartwheel over the graves of all his children. It's the message that what we think is lost is really found, that what we think is gone hasn't even begun yet, that there's something more than we imagine beyond what we see. Cartwheeling over a grave defies what appears to be the last word and dares to believe that what you think you see isn't real. It's a kick in the shins of darkness — sticking out your tongue at a tormentor. It's the same as turning the other cheek.

You can't let a blow change what you know about yourself and your world despite the humiliating, dehumanizing intention of the slap. Even when the slap seems as final as death.

Before physical death occurs, most of us will live through other deaths. Dreams die, relationships die. When it happens, remember, death has no sting left; it's a wasp without a stinger. Just another ugly pest.

Making It Mine

Easter arrives with the message that death has lost its staying power. Death as we know it isn't the last word. Hold on to your seat; there's more to come. St. Paul paraphrases the Old Testament prophet Hosea when he writes, "Where, O death, is your victory? Where, O death, is your sting?" Hear that? That's the sound of a tired but radically happy and utterly convinced saint sticking his tongue out at death.

There's an old Christmas television special about Rudolph and one of Santa's helpers who aspires to dentistry. Rudolph and the dentist wanna-be trudge out in the cold feeling like "misfits." With a few "misfit" friends the pair encounter various adversities including a fang-endowed abominable snowman with a nasty attitude. The beast is exceptionally eager to chomp down on the elf-dentist and his friends. There is no escaping its vicious jaws. Heroically, the little elf goes over a cliff taking the fanged brute with him to a snowy death and saving his friends. Sadly Rudolph and the others return to Santa's castle.

But that's not the end of the story. In a blaze of glory the elf shows up at Santa's door waving his dentist's pliers and riding the now toothless beast, made harmless by the hand of the elf.

This is what Christ has shown us about death: its teeth have been pulled. Death still bites, but the bite doesn't amount to much. Before physical death occurs, most of us will live through other deaths. Dreams die, relationships die. When it happens, remember, death has no sting left; it's a wasp without a stinger. Just another ugly pest.

Years ago I was the director of an Easter pageant. We knew our young Jesus had a flair for the dramatic. I had seen it during rehearsals. However, even I was surprised when our robed angels pushed back the cardboard "rock" and our eight-year-old Jesus made a single leap out of his grave, slid Vegas-style to land on one knee, arms spread out, and shouted, "Ta-da!"

That's the spirit of Easter: playful, alive, relentless — cartwheeling over graves and grinning in the face of death without so much as a blink. Ta-da!

Prayer Starter

May God be gracious to us and bless us
  and make his face shine upon us,
that your ways may be known on earth,
  your salvation among all nations.
May the peoples praise you, O God;
  may all the peoples praise you.

Psalm 67:1-3

Holy Spirit, Giver of Life, already I've known deaths and loss. It's still early in this life so I can count on more. Help me look beyond what I see and believe in what I don't see. Fill me with the promise of empty tombs, new beginnings, second chances, and eternal life with you.

# Soul Writing

What loss or death have you felt most deeply? Imagine that Jesus is living through that loss as your companion, takes the loss, and attaches it to himself on Good Friday and then emerges on Easter Sunday. Write about how you experience the loss now.

12

It's Time to Dance Your Dance
Something to Think About

I danced in the morning when the world was begun,
And I danced in the moon and stars and the sun.
I came down from heaven and I danced on the earth,
At Bethlehem I had my birth.

I danced for the scribe and the Pharisee,
But they would not dance and they wouldn't follow me.
I danced for fishermen, for James and John;
They came with me and the dance went on.

Dance, dance, wherever you may be!
I am the Lord of the dance, said he —
And I'll lead you all wherever you may be,
And I'll lead you all in the dance, said he.

I danced on the Sabbath and I cured the lame.
The holy people said it was a shame.
They whipped and they stripped and they hung me high;
They left me there on a cross to die.

I danced on a Friday when the sky turned black.
It's hard to dance with the devil on your back.
They buried my body and they thought I'd gone,
But I am the dance and I still go on!

Dance, dance, wherever you may be!
I am the Lord of the dance, said he ––
And I'll lead you all wherever you may be,
And I'll lead you all in the dance, said he.

They cut me down, but I leapt up high.
I am the life that will never, never die.
I'll live in you if you live in me,
I am the Lord of the dance, said he.
Dance, dance, wherever you may be!
I am the Lord of the dance, said he.
And I'll lead you all wherever you may be,
And I'll lead you all in the dance, said he.

— Sydney Carter*

We all made room

for Courtney's

dance; we knew

there would never

be another like it.

But isn't that true of

your dance, your

friends' dance, and

the dance of the kid

who is always the

outcast? There'll

never be another

dance like it.

*Excerpted from *Lord of the Dance* by Sydney Carter, copyright © 1963 by Stainer & Bell Ltd.;
all rights reserved; used by permission of Hope Publishing Co., Carol Stream, IL 60188

Making It Mine

Courtney was seventeen when I met her in a Celtic dance class. Her long arms and legs seemed to become one with music when we practiced. It was always hard to concentrate on my own practicing when I watched Courtney. We had a ritual. She stood next to me and stretched her long arms and I stepped a little to the right to make room for her. I moved gladly for the joy of dancing beside Courtney. I had as much right to my dance space as Courtney and she never crowded me either. We understood each other and we honored the other's dance.

Then Courtney stopped coming to class. No one knew why. After a few weeks we didn't talk about it. I heard from some young friends that Courtney had bone cancer. About six months later I saw her at the wedding of a mutual friend. Courtney was in a wheelchair. The young man with her was the love of her life since fifth grade, tall and slim and bright-eyed like Courtney; they could have passed for brother and sister.

As the band pumped up the music into the sort of rollicking rock we hear at weddings, he swung her wheelchair out to the dance floor. She laughed and cried as they wheeled about the floor, her arms taking up the rhythm with the magic I had always seen in her.

We all made room for Courtney's dance; we knew there would never be another like it. But isn't that true of your dance, your friends' dance, and the dance of the kid who is always the outcast? There'll never be another dance like it. So take to the floor. Dance, dance, wherever you may be....

Prayer Starter

I lift up my eyes to the hills —
   where does my help come from?
My help comes from the Lord,
   the Maker of heaven and earth.
He will not let your foot slip —
   he who watches over you will not slumber.

Psalm 121:1-3

Dear Lord, it's not easy learning to dance — what to do with my feet, where to put them, where to let them take me, what dance to take up as my own, and how to honor the dance of others. You lead. I will always need you to lead me in the dance.

Soul Writing

Think about your life as a unique dance that no one has ever danced before and will never dance again. Do I honor my dance? Do I honor the dance of other people? When you think about dancing as the whole of your life, you feel_____.

13
Would You Lie Down in This Fire?

Something to Think About

Norman Maclean, best known for the memoir A River Runs
Through It, *which was made into a fine movie, wrote a book about
the tragic deaths of fifteen young firefighters who belonged to the
United States Forest Service's elite group called smoke jumpers. They
were killed in the Mann Gulch in the Montana wilderness in a fire
that didn't behave the way smoke jumpers had been trained to expect
fires to behave.*

Like the smoke
jumpers at risk of
their lives, our best
chance for survival
is to lie down in
the fire by our
own choice.

While Sallee was cooling his lungs, he looked down and back at
Dodge and the crew and for the first time realized why Dodge had lit
his fire [this is a second fire begun by the leader of the group].

"I saw Dodge jump over the burning edge of the fire he had set
and saw him waving his arms and motioning for the other boys to
follow him. At that instant I could see what I believe was all the
balance of the crew. They were within twenty to fifty feet of Dodge and
just outside the burning edge of the fire Dodge had set. The last I
recall seeing the group of boys, they were angling up the slope in the
unburned grass and fairly close to the burning edge of the fire Dodge
had set....

"They didn't seem to pay any attention. That is the part I didn't
understand. They seemed to have something on their minds — all
headed in one direction."

He [Dodge] wet his handkerchief from his canteen, put it over his
mouth, and lay face down on the ground.... Even if the crew's training
had included a section on ... [how to] escape fires, it is not certain
that the crew would have listened to Dodge, would have entered the
fire and buried their faces in the ashes....

[Dodge] lived by lying in the ashes of his escape fire until the main
fire swept over him and cooled enough to let him stand up and brush
himself off....

From *Young Men and Fire* by Norman Maclean

Making It Mine

Dodge was foreman of that smoke jumpers crew. He was trying to save the lives of his crew from a fire that was jumping and flashing unpredictably. The young men were experienced parachute jumpers who dived into fires out of airplanes. They were fearless, a bit reckless, and, most agree, had little training in what to expect from a fire.

They didn't understand that their best chance of survival was to lie down in a fire to escape a fire. That's what Dodge was doing, but it didn't make sense to the boys running for their lives. One of those who survived said that even if he had seen the principle of an escape fire explained to him on a blackboard, he's not sure he would have followed Dodge into that fire either. He thinks he would have but wasn't sure.

Jesus called people to follow him too. His way of life is one that doesn't make sense to most people. The Christian values of loving, giving, serving, sacrificing, honesty — these are considered about as foolish and risky as lying down in a fire that you've set yourself. You've probably heard such ideas called self-debasing, self-degrading — things only losers would believe. We're told to look out for number one, never let anyone take advantage of you, do unto others before they do unto you.

Christ is calling us to something that looks risky and maybe even stupid, like lying face down in those ashes. And, like the smoke jumpers at risk of their lives, our best chance for survival is to lie down in the fire by our own choice. It's not always easy to believe that the seeming death he's calling us to is the only way to live. Lots of people are looking for another option. Faith means following anyway.

Prayer Starter

My heart is steadfast, O God;
   I will sing and make music with all my soul.
Awake, harp and lyre!
   I will awaken the dawn.

Psalm 108:1-2

Lord Jesus, I believe that my fulfillment lies in the same direction yours did — in surrender to the Father's will. But this is hard to take. Where are you taking me? What will others say? These are real questions. Show me the answers. Help me keep following. Give me a heart that is firmly fixed.

Soul Writing

Think about what happens inside you when you have a chance to talk about how your faith affects your daily life. How do you feel when the subject of Christianity or Church comes up in conversation? Are you concerned about what others might think of you? Which concerns are prudent? Which flow from fear?

14
A Grinning Panther with Charles Manson's Eyes
Something to Think About

Bob lives on the edge of polite society harboring immense hatred for those who label him an outcast. He talked about someone who had hurt a friend; he said the guy didn't deserve to live. Bob made a pistol of his hand, lifted it to his temple, and said, "Bam!"

So… this was going to be my companion for a two-hour flight. He was too tall for the narrow slot between seats, so his long legs spilled over into the aisle. His glossy shoulder-length black hair resembled a panther's coat; one streak of silver crossed his eyebrow and cheek. He wore a full beard, at least ten inches long, with the most recent growth showing gray. His skin was leathery and tan, his eyes the color of the Colorado mountain sky, bluer than even Disney animators can create, and his teeth were perfectly shaped, straight and white as he grinned up at me. A grinning panther dressed in black jeans, a black T-shirt, and flannel.

Something in those eyes reminded me of pictures of Charles Manson — only more striking and beautiful.

"That's my seat," I said, pointing to the window.

"Here, little lady, let me help you with that." He stood up, towering over me at what had to be close to seven feet tall. I relinquished my carry-on bag, sat down, and focused on the novel I intended to read.

He introduced himself. Bob. From Denver (we were leaving Denver) going to Michigan (my home) to visit his best friend whom he hadn't seen in several years. I didn't offer my name.

The woman in front of us tried to talk with Bob, saying things like he reminded her of her brother, generally trying to convince him that she was okay with how he looked and acted. I couldn't help smiling. That usually means someone is not okay with how you look or act. Bob used a rather graphic profanity in response to her blatantly condescending attitude.

She turned around with a whirl and an in-drawn breath. Bob noticed me noticing and said, "Yeah?" one eyebrow raised.

"You didn't have to be rude. It doesn't impress me." I looked back to the book.

He laughed and threw his head back. It was a low laugh, unmenacing, nice.

"Well, little lady, I won't try to impress you," he said.

A few minutes later Bob was playing with the phone on the back of the seat. He pushed buttons, rattled the phone, swore with skill …

then began making calls. No one was home; he left messages all over. Finally, he dialed a number and got a person.

His mother. My impression was he had not talked with her in a long time. At the end of the conversation he said (I paraphrase, since this too was splashed liberally with profanity), "I know last time I was home I was really messed up and I know how much it hurt you and my little girl. I'm not coming back until I get my act together; I won't put you through that again.... Mom, I love you." He hung up after the "I love you" as if he couldn't bear to hear her response.

I couldn't sit beside Bob pretending I hadn't heard. Bob deserved more. I looked up from my book. He was watching me again. The madness in those eyes was still evident, but so were the tears on his highly carved cheeks.

"You have kids, little lady?" he asked softly.

I told him I did.

"Some mothers ... well, they don't do their best ... but you can't blame them for that — isn't always their fault; they have their own demons, you know?"

Bob and I talked the rest of the flight. Now understand, Bob is the kind of guy mothers warn their kids to avoid. His language never improved. He believed in anarchy as a way of life. Bob lives on the edge of polite society harboring immense hatred for those who label him an outcast. He talked about someone who had hurt a friend; he said the guy didn't deserve to live. Bob made a pistol of his hand, lifted it to his temple, and said, "Bam!"

"What if it was one of your kids, or your mother, or your man?" Hurt, he meant; what if someone had hurt someone I loved?

"I'd be angry. But I don't think I'd be violent."

"You've never wanted revenge?"

"I didn't say that — I know how to hate, but I'm not proud of it and I think human beings are capable of more."

"All we need is love?" he sang softly and looked up at the airplane ceiling.

"Something like that."

"You know, little lady, you're okay. I wish I could believe like you do, but you'd get your throat cut in my world believing all we need is love."

Before we got to our connecting flight, after two hours of telling the story of his life, Bob said, "You're my sister. If you ever need anything, call me. I'll be there." He scribbled down his phone number and handed it to me. His sister? I had not even told him my name. I would never use that phone number.

We walked to the commuter flight together but were seated separately. He was about three rows ahead of me, on the aisle. I was jammed in next to a guy in a suit and female companion. When she sat down she sniffed and shuffled, making motions toward Bob as if he had no right to share the planet space with her.

He struck one long stare at her, turned his eyes on me, grinned and winked, then threw his head back and laughed — a much more menacing laugh this time. I had seen something wounded and tender in those stunning blue eyes, but it had been extinguished.

The flight lasted only twenty minutes. All the time I simmered in fury that this woman would dare judge Bob. No angel "my brother" Bob, not even likable, but deeply and profoundly human.

Then I remembered my own initial reaction to Bob: dread and resentment.

Off the plane, as my husband met me at the gate, I looked around for Bob. I wanted to somehow communicate that I was proud to be his "sister." We walked toward the escalator and then I saw him, hugging a shorter guy, bald, muscled, thirtyish. Across the terminal I called, "Bob!"

He had every right to ignore me. I shouldn't have sat quietly while the good citizens treated him like dirt. I wouldn't have blamed Bob if he had kept walking. But he didn't.

I motioned him over and said, "Bob, I want you to meet my husband. Honey, this is the angel who watched over me during the entire flight." Bob stood taller yet, dropped one flanneled arm over my shoulder and squeezed as he said, "Yeah, man, I took care of your old lady. She's something special; hell, you know that, don't you? I'd be proud to be her guardian angel anytime." My husband thanked him while shaking the hand of the grinning big panther.

I looked into the madness and warmth of Bob's eyes for the last time, stretched up on tiptoe, and kissed one leathery whiskered cheek. "Go in peace, brother," I whispered. He squeezed me hard and was gone.

I have no delusions about that interlude. Bob is out there somewhere shocking and irritating the good citizens still. God didn't send Bob to me so I could play missionary. No, Bob was my angel bearing the message that there remains a glimmer of humanity alive in the most unexpected places.

All these years into being a Christian, I'm still capable of making snap judgments. I'm not so different from the good citizens who sniff the air as Bob breezes past. I'm not so different from Bob. After all, he's my brother.

Making It Mine

"Them" and "Us." The cry of Hitler, of racists, of history's great haters has been the conviction that "they" are different from "us." But ordinary people believe this too. I was once involved in a church that was struggling against racial bigotry. One day a man rose up and challenged our efforts at reconciliation with, "You people just don't get it! They're different than us. Their morals are different. They aren't like us at all!"

In families where abuse is happening, people stop calling each other by name. They subtly take away the humanity of the other by not giving them a name. The adult perpetrators almost always refer to the victims as "the child" or "the kid" or just "him" or "her." When I counsel such people, I insist they use the child's name. They don't get away with saying, "… and then I hit the boy." They must say, "And then I hit Tommy." When they name Tommy, healing can begin.

Prayer Starter

Will you not revive us again,
    that your people may rejoice in you?
Show us your unfailing love, O Lord,
    and grant us your salvation.
I will listen to what God the Lord will say;
    he promises peace to his people,…

Psalm 85:6-8a

Father of us all, stop me when I don't look deep enough into someone else. Rattle me when I judge, condemn, and label. I name my prejudice and blindness. Forgive me and turn my heart toward you.

# Soul Writing

Jot down words you use for groups of "them" — people outside your immediate circle of friends and family. Hippies. Jews. Dopers. Feminists. Blacks. Now jot down the names of people you know who belong to these groups.

15
Looking for a Change?

Something to Think About

Once upon a time there was a prince who did what princes always do and fell in love with a fair maiden. But he had enemies, and one of them kidnaped the girl, holding her captive in a distant, very high tower.

The prince, clever boy that he was, developed a plan to rescue his fair maiden. He recruited the help of two common little creatures to help him. First, there was Claude the Caterpillar. Claude was a nice guy and didn't mind helping fair maidens and their desperate prince-types. But Claude was, well … sort of crusty. He was the kind of person that, upon your meeting him in the morning, would make you wonder, "What's wrong with him? Must have gotten up on the wrong side of bed this morning."

Anyway, the prince enlisted Claude to get a message to Ms. Fair Maiden. Claude took the message and began inching his way along toward the tower. Being a fat little caterpillar he had to work hard, even sweat some. "Wouldn't you know it," he mumbled, "the sun would pick today to shine and here I am sweating and steamy."

Just then the weather changed; clouds and rain moved. "Rain, of all things," he grumbled, "and I just had this suit cleaned." But Claude wasn't a quitter. He made it to the tower, searched for a way up, and then inched up, effort upon effort, only to discover the vine he had found was a rosebush complete with thorns. All the way up the tower you could hear, "Ouch, ah, ow, ouch, ouch…." Finally he came to the ledge of the window and heaved himself up where Fair Maiden was watching him rather curiously.

Between the lies
and alibis
There's an honesty
that's warm
and bold/
Under that cold
shoulder
There's a
heart of gold

"Hey, lady! What are you looking at? Are you Fair Maiden in Distress? Well, you don't look all that distressed to me."

She looked down at the muddy, sweaty, annoyed caterpillar a bit startled and thought what a rude little thing he was.

Claude gave her another once-over and said, "You're kidding. You mean I came all the way up here for the likes of you? Oh, well, probably not much of a prince either. Listen up: He sent a message. You wouldn't believe how hard it's been getting it here. His message — are you listening? — nod your head or something, would you? The message is 'Get ready.' He's coming to get you, at five sharp. Understand? All right. Good. I'm out of here." And off he went, ouching all the way to the bottom of the tower.

Next, the prince sent Barney Butterfly. Barney was not so sure of himself with the rain and wind but said he'd try. His delicate wings flapped against the winds as he fought to stay in the air, back and forth, blasted by rain all the way to the tower window. Just as he spotted the window, a bird swooped down to take him in one bite, and he flew into the window in a desperate state with the bird after him.

Ms. Fair Maiden shooed away the bird, striking his beak sharply. She reached out her hand to Barney, who landed on it and took a deep breath.

She brought him close, and he was glad for her warmth and safety. "Fair Maiden, I have a message from your prince, who loves you dearly. At the sound of his voice jump out the window and into his arms. He'll never let you hit the ground."

The maiden smiled. "Thank you, Butterfly. You're very kind, brave even. Do you by chance know that cranky caterpillar? Why would he bring such good news in such a nasty manner?"

The butterfly fluttered, drying his wings. "Oh, you've met Claude. Well, that's just Claude. Don't pay him any attention. I used to be that way too, until I was transformed."

 # Making It Mine

Wild Heart
Somewhere in the empty stare
There is a look of love
Behind that suit of angry armor
There is a gentle dove
Between the lies and alibis
There's an honesty that's warm and bold
Under that cold shoulder
There's a heart of gold....
Wild Heart
Something's changing you....

Written by Gordon Kennedy and Randy Holland; recorded for Sparrow by Phil Keaggy (reproduction prohibited, used by permission)

Prayer Starter

Have mercy on me, O God,
   according to your unfailing love;
according to your great compassion
   blot out my transgressions.
Wash away all my iniquity
   and cleanse me from my sin.

Psalm 51:1-2

Lord Jesus Christ, teach me to name what is dark in myself, to call it sin and run to you for help. Don't let me be overwhelmed with regret but hopeful and at peace in your love for me. I need to change. Help me believe you are changing me.

Soul Writing

Write about the ways you would most like to change. What prevents you from changing? What is the most drastic personal transformation you know of? Write about it.

16
"Don't Quit — Keep Playing"

Something to Think About

A mother who wanted to encourage her little boy's interest in the piano took him to a concert by the great Paderewski. They arrived early at the majestic concert hall because there was no reserved seating. Waiting for the master's hand was a magnificent Steinway piano centered on the long stage. The mother and her son took seats close to the stage. Before long, friends joined them and the mother was distracted talking to the person next to her. The boy slipped away.

At eight o'clock, the lights in the auditorium dimmed, spotlights struck the stage, and only then did the mother notice her son. He sat on the bench of the Steinway, innocently and with contentment picking out "Twinkle, Twinkle, Little Star."

Before the stunned and embarrassed parent could retrieve her son, Paderewski appeared on stage and strode over to the piano. He leaned down to the boy and reached an arm around each side of him. He whispered to the boy: "Don't quit — keep playing."

With his left hand the master pianist began filling in the bass. Soon his right hand improvised obligato. Before an amused, shocked, and delighted audience the old master and the young novice filled the concert hall with unforgettable music. The crowd was mesmerized.

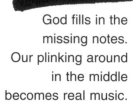

God fills in the missing notes. Our plinking around in the middle becomes real music. The melodies we struggle to play are transformed beyond our wildest dreams by God, and music happens.

Making It Mine

Much of what we try to accomplish in our short lives appears to us to be little more than a plinking out of empty notes. Our very best attempts fall short. The problems facing humanity are so big that the little efforts you and I make can hardly seem worthwhile. Someone said that all of us have a symphony we can play with our lives, "… but most of us die with the music still inside."

Our lives, unpolished as they might be, are still surrounded by God, who whispers to us over and over, "Don't quit — keep playing." And as we do exactly that, somehow God fills in the missing notes. Our plinking around in the middle becomes real music. The melodies we struggle to play are transformed beyond our wildest dreams by God, and music happens. It works.

Our part: stay at the keyboard. Rest in the arms that are big enough to make up for anything you might lack. Cooperate. Obey. Don't stop playing. Never quit. The music will happen.

Prayer Starter

Show me your ways, O Lord,
  teach me your paths;
guide me in your truth and teach me,
  for you are God my Savior,
  and my hope is in you all day long.

Psalm 25:4-5

Master, it's hard to believe that anything I do could make any kind of difference. Here I am, one person with my handful of dreams and convictions. Maybe all I can really do is keep trying and saying, "Here I am."

Soul Writing

Is there something you're involved with right now that you're ready to give up on? How could faith help you "keep playing"?

17
"Life Is Not Fair"

Something to Think About

A mother writes of her two sons.

Randy is the older son. He has a kind of dynamism, a star aura. When he was born, after a prolonged and complicated labor and delivery, the doctor held him up. He had eye contact with me and the assembled medical personnel, and smiled ... he was born smiling.

When he was playing Little League Baseball, he had been playing two years and had never had a good hit.... One night it came. On the first pitch over the plate he swung and hit it: CRACK! Over the fence! He took off running: first base, second, third.... Rounding third, he took off his hat and bowed to the fans who had always known it was only a matter of time. As he crossed the plate, the umpire said, "Son, you're out. You threw your bat."

Two innings later Randy was up again. The same thing happened. The first pitch: CRACK! Over the fence. He took off running. The umpire took off after him. He caught him by his jersey near first base.

"Son, look at your bat! You're OUT!"

In his euphoria that he had pulled it off yet another time, Randy had really let the bat go. It was near third base ... I could plainly see my Randy's face. All the color drained from it, which is when I discovered that rage is white and not red. I waited. I knew his vocabulary. I knew he would probably be banned from competitive sports.... He jammed his hands down in his pockets. Thirty full seconds went by. And then he said, "Yes sir," and went to the dugout.

"Randy, can I talk to you about the game?"

"I guess so, Mom."

"... What you know is something many people don't learn until they are much older ... life is not fair."

A corollary happened a few weeks later. Boo, the youngest, was having his game. It was his second year playing for the same team, and the second year they put him on the bench for three quarters of the game.... The coach and his wife seemed to me to run the team like a setting for the diamond who was their son. The coach's wife was a Supermom, Ex-Miss America type woman. When Boo came up to bat for the first time, she got up and went to the concession stand.

This night the pitcher threw a pitch that hit the bat right above

"God is
a loving presence
in our lives,
but God isn't an
insurance policy ...
life is good,
but life is not fair."

his hands. It dribbled off into the grass and Boo took off. The pitcher was so stunned that by the time he picked it up Boo had slid around second base and never stopped. The pitcher overthrew at third and Boo came home.

The crowd went wild. The coach's wife came back.

"What happened?" she asked me.

I looked right into her Supermom, Ex-Miss America face and said: "Boo hit a home run."

The flip side of *life is not fair* is that sometimes *we get incredible breaks in our favor*.... Life is mixed.

Adapted from *Lessons of the Heart* by Patricia Livingston

Making It Mine

Anna was one of those kids you just know is going straight to the top. She held a steady 4.0 GPA in high school. Everyone liked her — even those who didn't agree with her. She was accepted at a great college. She had scholarships. She was on her way.

In December of her senior year Anna became ill. Really ill. It developed into pneumonia. This was back when pneumonia wasn't as easily treated. She spent six weeks in the hospital — fighting for her life.

When she came back, she tackled school and all the work with a gusto. Those of us who knew her worried that she'd make herself sick again. She didn't. She grew stronger every day and by April she was caught up, as if she hadn't missed a beat. Head of the class. We were all so proud of her. She gave us hope.

Once, during lunch around a lunchroom table, one of the guys who had fallen behind in school because of family complications said, "But I keep thinking if Anna can do it I can too. You know, things are hard right now, but it's nothing like she faced and she's going to be valedictorian."

The next day Anna's father had a heart attack. He died before the ambulance could get to him, in the arms of Anna's mother. Talk about family complications. Anna was devastated. And everything changed. She couldn't bring herself to leave her mother and two younger brothers to run the family business, tie up all the loose ends, and get through the very difficult time alone.

But she had worked so hard. She had overcome so much. She had plans; she was ready to get on with her life. It wasn't fair. Anna never did get to college. She dreamed of being a symphony director. She isn't. But she isn't bitter. She still runs the family business. She's very happy.

Sometimes we get incredible breaks. Sometimes we don't. I was once at a church picnic where a college-age couple pulled their three-year-old daughter out of the pond. In the three minutes she had been out of their sight, she had drowned. When I saw the child's father many years later, he had gone through a real crisis of faith but had concluded, "God is a loving presence in our lives, but God isn't an insurance policy … life is good, but life is not fair."

Prayer Starter

Blessed are those whose strength is in you,
 who have set their hearts on pilgrimage.
They go from strength to strength,
 till each appears before God in Zion.
For the Lord God is a sun and shield;
 the Lord bestows favor and honor.

Psalm 84:5, 7, 11a

Lead, kindly light, amid the encircling gloom,
Lead thou me on;
The night is dark, and I am far from home;
Lead thou me on;
Keep thou my feet; I do not ask to see
The distant scene: one step [is] enough for me.

— *John Henry Newman*

Soul Writing

Sometimes we pray with clenched fists and wet faces. Write about a time when something seemed very unfair. How could praying these prayers help?

18
God Is:
(a) The Vegetable Man;
(b) The Lion; (c) Both

Something to Think About

Josh was the old man next door. He raised his own chickens, sold eggs, planted his own garden, and sold vegetables. I was afraid of Josh when I was a child. He was always stooped over when he walked. He could not speak many words in English. I once saw him chop off the head of one of his chickens. Josh didn't have many teeth.

One early September morning my mother asked me if I would run down to Josh's and buy some tomatoes. My mother wanted to add some flavor to her stew. I had never walked to Josh's house alone before…. Always an obedient boy, I did as my mother asked. My mother handed me a dollar to pay for the tomatoes. After I stood before Josh's house for a long time, I pulled the string of the bell that hung from the front door.

"Yes?" he asked as he opened the door and looked at me.

"My mother would like two tomatoes." I wanted to run.

"In the back." Josh closed the door, and by the time I stepped to the back of his house, he was already there standing beside his vegetable stand. I watched as he reached over with his big hands and lifted four tomatoes and placed them into a brown bag. He reached down and handed me the bag. "No charge."

I looked up at him, and he smiled, revealing his few teeth and his good heart…. Sometimes we think God is a frightening power that oversees all that we do with a gruff cast of his eye. Like a child confronting the strong, old vegetable man, we can sometimes be intimidated by the truth and mystery of God's love for us, but then his infinite kindness is revealed….

From *Simple Wonders* by Christopher DeVinck

Along with our weekly bulletins and missals at Church we should also receive crash helmets just in case God decides to answer all our pleadings and show up some Sunday.

Making It Mine

In a children's story written by C. S. Lewis, *The Lion, The Witch and the Wardrobe*, Lucy, a young girl, is about to run into Aslan, the Great Lion. She asks Mr. Beaver what Aslan is like.

"Is — Is he a man?" asked Lucy.

"Aslan a man!" said Mr. Beaver sternly. "Certainly not. I tell you he is the King … Aslan is a lion — The Lion, the Great Lion."

"… Is he — quite safe? I shall feel rather nervous about meeting a lion."

"Safe!?" Said Mr. Beaver. "Don't you hear…. Who said anything about safe? 'Course he isn't safe. But he's good."

Annie Dillard, novelist, has suggested that along with our weekly bulletins and missals at Church we should also receive crash helmets just in case God decides to answer all our pleadings and show up some Sunday.

Poet Emily Dickinson compared our lives to being harnessed in a carriage behind wild, fast racing horses — her image of God. Wild. Beautiful. Harnessed tight.

God isn't safe. But God is indeed good. Very good.

Prayer Starter

Give thanks to the Lord, for he is good;
   his love endures forever.
The Lord is God,
   and he has made his light shine upon us.
With boughs in hand, join in the festal procession
   up to the horns of the altar.
You are my God, and I will give you thanks;
   you are my God, and I will exalt you.

Psalm 118:1, 27-28

Tie the strings to my life, my Lord,
Then I am ready to go!
Just a look at the horses,
Rapid! That will do!…

But never I mind the bridges
And never I mind the sea;
Held fast in everlasting race
By my own choice and thee….

— Emily Dickinson

 # Soul Writing

Think about how God can be both like the kind vegetable man and Aslan the Lion. Which image of God is most familiar to you? In what situations might each image of God be a source of strength and comfort for you?

19
Homesick

Something to Think About

Lines from various songs tell us a lot about the longings of human hearts.

"Feels like home to me ... feels like I'm on my way back where I belong ..." (Bonnie Raitt).

"There's a place for us, somewhere a place for us ... we'll find a new way of living, we'll find a way of forgiving ... "(West Side Story).

"Somewhere over the rainbow bluebirds fly, birds fly over the rainbow ... why can't I ..." (Wizard of Oz).

"I've never gone so far that I've forgotten my way home, the best things always bring you back again, over and over ..." (Russ Taft).

From *Between the Dreaming and the Coming True: The Road Home to God* by Robert Benson:

This is what I believe. We were with God in the beginning. I do not understand that exactly — what we looked like, what we did all day, how we got along, any of it. Then we were sent here. And I am not sure that I understand that very well, either. And I believe we are going home to God someday, and what that will be like is as much a mystery to me as any of the rest of it.... But I believe those things are true and that what we have here on earth in between is a longing — for the God that we have known and for the God we are going home to.

We're in a waiting room — all of us together — learning about living and dying and loving. We're on our way home.

Making It Mine

We're in a waiting room on the fifth floor of a children's hospital. This particular floor is dedicated to the treatment of children with cancer. In the waiting room a collection of children and teens wait for their turn to have chemicals put into their veins in the hope of arresting the deadly spread of cancer. Parents, relatives, and friends are with the kids as they wait. I'm there with my six-month-old daughter, who has a malignant tumor in her arm and shoulder.

It's never spoken, but we have something like assigned seating in the place. And today one of the chairs is empty. We know what that means. Another one is gone. Another one has lost. We're very quiet today.

Next to me is Matthew's mother. Matthew is a year old. He's much too thin for a year-old child, with sticks for arms and legs. He has the largest eyes I've ever seen on a child. He's bald. Chemo does that.

Across from Matthew is a young teenaged girl. She's wearing a stocking cap to cover her head. She's been here a long time and she looks tired. She's curled up in her chair in something like a fetal position. Her aunt is with her today.

Matthew's mother puts him on the floor. He pulls himself up, lets go of the chair, and just stands there wobbling. We're all watching. When a child like Matthew does something as ordinary as learn to walk, it's good news in this place. It's a sign of hope.

The girl watches. She doesn't want us to know she's watching him, though. She unfolds her thin arms and legs. Matthew's sky-blue gaze fixes on the girl. He waves both arms and he takes off walking, really walking, while his mother beams at this never-before-seen feat. He takes seven wobbly steps to the girl. I count them. He bumps into her knees, slaps his hands down on her legs, and looks up at her with a great big grin and grunt of triumph.

Magic. She smiles. She speaks. Another first.

"Can I hold him?"

"Sure."

She scoops the boy into her arms, "Well, Mr. Matthew, aren't you something!" she says softly and presses him tight to her caved-in chest. He relaxes against her, his head under her chin and his arms wide open around her shoulders. He takes a deep breath and exhales. They sit like that a few minutes.

It's hard to tell who's holding whom. But they've come home to each other.

We know in a way very few people ever know that we all belong to one another in this world. In our living and dying we're so alike. It's the same sense I have when I walk in an old cemetery or watch the light of recognition in the eighty-eight-year-old eyes of my great aunt when she sees me. There's a knowing that we are part of some bigger Whole. We belong to one another.

We're in a waiting room — all of us together — learning about living and dying and loving. We're on our way home. Before we get there, we'll see amazing sights here in the waiting room. Let's share them.

Prayer Starter

As a father has compassion on his children,
    so the Lord has compassion on those who fear him;
for he knows how we are formed,
    and he remembers that we are dust.
But from everlasting to everlasting
    the Lord's love is with those who fear him,
    and his righteousness with their children's children.

Psalm 103:13-14, 17

God of love and Father of us all, bless our attempts at loving one another and living together in community. Give us patience and understanding. Give us open arms and hearts. You who are always faithful to us, teach me to love with an undivided heart.

 # Soul Writing

Have you ever experienced homesickness — an overpowering desire to go home, to be back with people who love you no matter what? Write about it. What did you feel? Have you felt a similar feeling about a group you were part of: a school, a club?

20
An Ordinary Hero

Something to Think About

A nameless, ordinary, man. His story is part of a bigger story you might remember, a news story about genocide in Rwanda, a country in East Africa. The news story is the typical kind of horror we've grown accustomed to hearing over our meat loaf and mashed potatoes, evening after evening — brutality, inhumanity, astounding cruelty. Maybe the real horror is that such stories are commonplace.

In Rwanda, Hutus butchered the Tutsis with machetes. They slaughtered old and young, adults and children, men and women. Hutus in charge ordered ordinary Hutus to kill all the Tutsis they could find. Their only crime was that they were Tutsis.

One man refused. When the order was given, this nameless Hutu refused to obey. Instead, he hid seventeen Tutsis and saved their lives.

Looking at him on television there's nothing special about him. He's so ordinary that his namelessness seems right. He could represent every person who has ever said no to the madness pressing in around them — a strong, determined *no* that isn't going to change because it's uncomfortable.

The Hutu man exhibited no signs of anger, rage, passion, defiance, or even pride in what he'd done. He didn't understand what the fuss was about. He had done the thing that seemed right, what human beings are supposed to do. He's the stuff saints, heroes, and martyrs are made of, and yet he's lost in the ordinary crowd. Saints lurk among us. We're not aware of them.

This man's courage is exceptional because he stood alone. Every other Hutu went about hacking their Tutsi neighbors to death, but he made a naked decision not to join in the madness. He chose to resist, and he chose it at obvious danger to himself. The ordinary human being at his ordinary best.

Making It Mine

Chances are, we aren't called upon to make such dramatic decisions about life and death, right and wrong. Not only are we "ordinary" people; most often our decisions to resist the tide when it is going the wrong way will seem pretty ordinary also. There's a little-noticed danger in the ordinariness of the choices we make day to day.

Decisions set us on certain paths. There's no way to know how your decision to take a certain path will impact the rest of your life or the lives of all the others you come in contact with.

We might start thinking that because our choices are ordinary ones they don't make a difference.

No one will notice one "little" lie.

No one will notice cheating on one test.

If I fail to do the "right" thing in this situation, it isn't going to hurt anyone and it won't impact the big picture.

Maybe. But maybe not. Decisions set us on certain paths. There's no way to know how your decision to take a certain path will impact the rest of your life or the lives of all the others you come in contact with. To be human means that we can't see tomorrow. But we can be sure that every act will have a reaction and every choice a consequence or result.

Someone once wrote: "We heap together the mistakes of our lives and call the monster Destiny." That's one way to live with the choices we make. Another, and a better one, I think, is to begin considering our decisions as the tools we use to cooperate with God in shaping our lives. In the Old Testament Scriptures, God is said to gather the people together and say, "I set before you this day life and death, blessings and cursings. Now choose life."

When we are making decisions, we are doing nothing ordinary. We are gathered before God with all the human race and charged to consider carefully the power, responsibility, and freedom to decide — and choose life.

 # Prayer Starter

For the Lord loves the just
   and will not forsake his faithful ones.
Consider the blameless, observe the upright;
   there is a future for the man of peace.
Psalm 37:28, 37

God, help me seize opportunities with courage when they come my way. Often the ways I can stand up for what's right just don't seem important. Make me hungry for what is right.

 **Soul Writing**

Think about a time you made a difficult decision to stand alone against something that was clearly wrong. Write about it. Where did you get courage?

21
A Father's Kiss

Something to Think About

A siren blasting into my brain made it difficult to clear away the hurting blur. Just before tumbling back into unconsciousness, I remembered the hayride. I hopped off the wagon to gather straw from the road for our rollicking hay fight. It was dark, and the wagon trudged slowly.

No headlights; no warning. I felt the heat of the car before the impact. My horrified friends witnessed the accident. They told me later I flew about twenty feet into the air and landed on the gravel road, face down. Small bits of dirt and rock were embedded in my sixteen-year-old face.

As I struggled for consciousness in the ambulance, my face felt dead; and it terrified me. "Not my face, God, no … not my face …" I prayed desperately.

I was proud of my looks. People related to me differently from the way they related to less-attractive girls. That had been true since childhood; and it was a lesson that I, like most cute children, learned early.

I remember one Sunday as we arrived at church. I was gathering my small purse, gloves, and missal. Dad opened the door. He extended his hand to me with a twinkle in his eye and said, "A hand, my lady?" Then he swept me up into his arms and told me how pretty I was and said, "No father has ever loved a little girl more than I love you."

I don't know what it was about that morning that so impressed me. In the heart of a child, one who didn't understand what a father's love really is, I thought it must have been the pretty dress, but most of all my prettiness, that Dad loved.

I was unable to open my eyes more than a slit the next morning when I asked a nurse for a mirror. She didn't look at my face as she took my blood pressure. Instead, she gazed at my arm and said, "You just concern yourself with getting well, young lady!"

Her refusal to give me a mirror fueled irrational determination. If she wouldn't give me a mirror, I reasoned, it must be worse than I imagined. My face felt tight and itchy. It burned sometimes and ached other times. I didn't touch it, though, because my doctor said that might cause infection.

As he looked into my battered face, his eyes filled with tears. Slowly Daddy leaned toward me; and with his eyes open, he gently kissed my scabbed, oozing lips.

My parents kept vigil at my bedside. They also battled with me to keep mirrors away. As my body healed internally and strength returned, I became increasingly difficult. On the fifth day, I demanded Dad give me a mirror. Angry and beaten down, he snapped, "Don't ask me again! I said no, and that's it!"

I propped myself up on my elbows and through lips that could barely move I hissed: "You don't love me. Now that I'm not pretty anymore, you just don't love me!"

Dad was stunned. He slowly lowered into a chair and put his head in his hands. His shoulders heaved. My mother walked over and put her hand on his shoulder and glared at me. I collapsed against the pillows. The room was quiet, filled with the soft sound of my father trying to control his tears.

I didn't ask my parents for a mirror again. Instead, I waited until someone was straightening out my room the next morning. I figured one of the housekeeping staff might not know about the "no mirror" order.

My curtain was drawn shut. From behind it, I asked for a mirror that "I must have mislaid." After a little searching, she found one and discreetly handed it to me around the curtain.

Nothing could have prepared me for the image that resembled a giant scraped knee, oozing and bright pink, looking out at me. My eyes and lips were crusted and swollen. Hardly a patch of skin, ear to ear, had escaped trauma.

A little while later my father arrived with magazines and homework tucked under his arm. He found me staring into the mirror.

He pried my fingers from around the mirror without mercy as he matter-of-factly said, "It isn't important. No one will love you less."

Finally he got the mirror away and tossed in into a chair. Then he sat on the edge of my bed, taking me into his arms.

"I know what you think," he said.

"You couldn't," I mumbled, turning away from him and staring out the window.

"You're wrong," he continued, ignoring my self-pity. "This will not change anything," he repeated. He put his hand on my arm, running it over an IV needle. "The people who love you have seen you at your worst, you know."

"Right. Seen me with rollers or with cold cream, not with my face ripped off!"

"Let's talk about me, then. I love you. Nothing will ever change that because it's you I love, not your outside. I've changed your diapers and watched your skin change to a cluster of blisters with chicken pox. I've wiped up your bloody noses and held your head while you threw up in the toilet.

"I've loved you when you weren't pretty," he hesitated and then continued. "Yesterday, you were ugly—not because of your skin either, but because you behaved ugly. But I'm here today, and I'll be here tomorrow. Fathers don't stop loving their children no matter what life takes away from them. You will be blessed if life takes only your face."

I turned to my father, feeling it was all words, spoken out of duty — polite lies. I looked at him through swollen eyes and spoke through bloody lips.

"Look at me then, Daddy. Look at me and tell me you love me!" My tone of voice and words defied and accused him.

I will never forget what happened next. As he looked into my battered face, his eyes filled with tears. Slowly Daddy leaned toward me; and with his eyes open, he gently kissed my scabbed, oozing lips.

It was the kiss that tucked me in every night of young life, the kiss that warmed each morning. My father's kiss was probably the one thing carrying the power to assure me that love doesn't change. It was a kiss echoing eternity.

All that remains of my accident today is one tiny indentation just above an eyebrow. But my father's kiss and all it taught me about love is still with me.

 Making It Mine

God's love has been most often compared to a father's love. But it's a father's love that acts an awful lot like what we think of as motherly love. Consider the parable of the prodigal son in the Bible, for example. The kid gets all full of himself and takes off. By taking his inheritance, he as much as says he wishes his father were dead. It's not the kind of thing Jewish fathers tolerated. It's not the kind of thing most fathers would put up with. But in the biblical story we encounter a father who not only lets it slip by, he runs to greet the rascal when he comes home hat in hand with his well-practiced sad story and apology on his lips.

The young man had shamed his father and family. Yet, there's the patriarch of the family, lifting his robes and running down the road to meet the returning brat. Today's experts would tell him a little "tough love" is in order. It's just not a "manly" thing to do.

A story from the local news retells this in modern terms. It's about a teenaged Midwestern girl with strict parents. They didn't like short skirts and loud music. She got fed up with her "overbearing" father and ran away, heading for the big city where she quickly declined until about two years later she was a homeless junkie and hooker. She came to herself, realizing that home hadn't been all that bad. She bought a bus ticket for home and she called her father from the bus station just before she left. But her parents weren't home. She left a message that said basically, "I was an idiot. I want to come home. If I'm welcome, meet me at the bus station; otherwise I'll get back on the bus and keep going."

When the girl arrived, countless relatives were waiting for her, waving banners and crying and opening their arms. Her father embraced her, took her home, and never derided her stupid behavior.

God is the kind of Father who throws parties for returning rebels and kisses lips that curse more often than they bless. Nothing you ever do will make God love you less; nothing you ever do will make God love you more. You're loved because you're his kid. Period.

 # Prayer Starter

I will sing of the Lord's great love forever;
> with my mouth I will make your faithfulness known through all
> > generations.
I will declare that your love stands firm forever,
> that you established your faithfulness in heaven itself.

Psalm 89:1-2

Lord Jesus Christ, I find it hard to believe that true love is given because of who I am and not how I look or what I own. I might believe it sometimes, but I often don't act that way. Give me eyes to see genuine love and good sense to stay away from the imitation.

Soul Writing

Reflect on the different ideas you have about love. Write them down. Where do they come from? What messages am I taking in from music, television, and movies about love? Do I know any models for love without strings attached?

22
Lessons from a Golden Retriever
Something to Think About

Things We Can Learn From A Dog (source unknown):

•Never pass up the opportunity to go for a joyride.

•Allow the experience of fresh air and wind in your face to be honest ecstasy.

•When loved ones show up, run to greet them, especially when they're coming home.

•Trust those who know more than you do and practice obedience to them.

•Let others know when your territory has been invaded.

•Take naps and stretch often.

•Run, romp, and play every chance you get, at least daily.

•Eat with gusto and enthusiasm. Be grateful to those who feed you.

•Be loyal.

•Never pretend to be what you aren't.

•If something you want is buried deep, dig until you find it.

•When someone is having a bad day, be silent, sit nearby, and nuzzle gently.

•Thrive on the loving attention you're given and let people who mean well touch you.

•Avoid biting when a simple growl will do.

•On hot days, drink lots of water and lie quietly under a shady tree.

•When you're happy, dance around with exuberance and wag your whole body.

•No matter how often you're scolded don't buy into the guilt thing and pout; run right back and make friends as fast as you can.

•Delight in simple joys: a long walk, cold water, having your hair brushed, throwing a ball with a friend, etc.

•Bond with your pack.

The secret to happiness is this — the sense that we live in a friendly universe where we get bumped and bruised every now and then by falling acorns.

Making It Mine

Remember the story of Chicken Little? A falling acorn hits Chicken Little's head, convincing her the sky is falling. She goes into a frenzy of doomsday announcements to all in earshot, "The sky is falling! The sky is falling!"

If Chicken Little had been a golden retriever she wouldn't have gone to pieces over the possibility of the sky falling. She would have done something far more sensible like taking one more romp with a kid or drinking another bowl of cold water or rushing to hold up the sky so it wouldn't fall on the owner she adored.

"The sky is falling!" is a way of life. Fear is exaggerated, and life is made into the sum total of all the frightening possibilities. Fear turns acorns into giant boulders crushing our pin-sized heads to dust.

The sky *is* immense and awe-inspiring. Life is like that. It's bigger than you can see. It goes off in directions you can't imagine. It clouds over, it clears; we see it brighten one moment only to glimpse lightning cut across it the next. It seems to change all the time, yet on some level we know it doesn't actually change. What we perceive as change is the same relentless cycle of seasons — life and death, light and dark — that humans have known since the beginning.

Golden retrievers, like children, instinctively know that the sky isn't rickety. Some mysterious trust gives them a sense of safety.

The secret to happiness is this — the sense that we live in a friendly universe where we get bumped and bruised every now and then by falling acorns. The One who holds the canopy over our heads can be trusted to keep it tacked up there generation after generation. Chicken Little needs to take a lesson about faith from dogs, and so do we. Just let an acorn be an acorn and rest at ease under the sturdy, ancient sky.

Prayer Starter

Those who look to him are radiant;
   their faces are never covered with shame.
Taste and see that the Lord is good;
   blessed is the man who takes refuge in him.

Psalm 34:5, 8

I thank you, Lord, for my being, my life, my gift of reason, for my nurture, my preservation, my guidance. I thank you for all the days of my life. Teach me to keep it simple.

Soul Writing

Write about some ways you can keep your life uncomplicated and restful? Do you have some "Chicken Little" kind of fears? What could you do today that would help you rest easier?

23

The Patron Saint of Failures and Other Humble Folk

Something to Think About

Solanus Casey (1870-1957) could easily be the definition that appears in the dictionary after the word, "humble" or maybe ... even "failure." He was a priest, but by contemporary standards his priestly vocation was a failure. He performed the same menial work day after day for forty years. But we're getting ahead of our story.

Casey witnessed a tragedy in 1891 that changed his life. He was not quite twenty-one, ambitious and hardworking. He had been a lumberjack, brick maker, prison guard, streetcar conductor. One afternoon, his streetcar rounded a corner and his life changed. He brought the streetcar to a screeching halt, narrowly missing a crowd of people. Casey wasn't prepared for the bloody scene he found. A drunken sailor stood cursing over a young woman he had just raped and stabbed repeatedly. The crowd was in a rage. The image was branded into his mind forever. He prayed daily for the girl, the sailor, the people in the crowd. That very year he entered the seminary in Wisconsin.

Casey wasn't much of a student. He needed to know both Latin and German to get by in the seminary and he knew neither. Eventually he was told to leave the seminary. He joined the Capuchin order in Detroit and spent seven years studying at the Capuchin seminary in Wisconsin. Once more German and Latin threatened him. His seminary professors opposed ordaining him. Finally, they agreed, but they limited his ministry. He would not be allowed to administer penance or preach formally. He wouldn't even be allowed to wear the Capuchin hood.

For fifty-three years Father Solanus would never hear a confession or conduct a retreat. He spent forty of those years answering the door of the monastery. Others would have complained; he did not. But this simple service launched a remarkable career as a spiritual director, friend, and miracle-worker. People reported amazing healings. The world rushed to the door of the monastery, eager for the prayers and love of Father Solanus.

The one considered not very smart and hardly worthwhile was used by God to touch literally thousands of lives. Others in Solanus's situation would have considered themselves outcasts and grown bitter.

The world rushed to the door of the monastery, eager for the prayers and love of Father Solanus. The one considered not very smart and hardly worthwhile was used by God to touch literally thousands of lives.

But Solanus Casey opened the door to the hungry at his doorstep. He didn't bother with thinking about what anyone else thought of him. He modestly and peacefully opened his heart, and his arms to life, just exactly as God had given it to him. He trusted.

 Making It Mine

I've heard a story about a brother and sister. The sister has a serious illness. She undergoes surgery. During surgery she begins to bleed heavily, threatening her life. She has a rare blood type; the hospital does not have blood on hand to transfuse her. The frantic doctors test everyone in the girl's family and discover that her five-year-old brother's blood matches hers. He's asked if he will donate blood to his sister and without a second thought he agrees.

The transfusion takes place without a hitch. He's told to stay in bed for a little while and is left alone. After about twenty minutes the nurse returns and the little guy asks, "When do I die?"

He believed he was giving his life for his sister. He did so because he was asked to. He wasn't old enough to understand the situation. He simply did what was needed because he had the ability to do it. He said yes to the situation and accepted the realities of the situation.

That's what Solanus Casey teaches us too. We will find ourselves in circumstances that don't turn out exactly as we planned. We'll fail at some things and we'll sometimes amaze ourselves with our success in unexpected ways.

To follow the will of God means making the most of the present situation. It means accepting that interruption, changes in plans, delay, or refusal may be part of God's will for you. What we think is an ending or a death could be something else — we don't always know, since we can't see the bigger picture. The best we can do is offer ourselves for whatever God wills. Then we just trust.

An author I know tells of a crisis in his life when it seemed highly unlikely that anything good could come of the circumstance. He was jogging one morning on a narrow road while preoccupied with worry. He's not the kind of guy who talks about religious experiences or his faith very easily. He heard a car come up behind him fast and as he stepped away from the highway it seemed to swerve and just barely missed him. As it sped away he noticed the license plate.

It read "Trust."

Nothing else. Just trust. Trust God. Trust yourself. Trust the universe. Trust. Sometimes it's the near misses that carry the message.

Prayer Starter

You who fear him, trust in the Lord —
    he is their help and shield.
May the Lord make you increase,
    both you and your children.
May you be blessed by the Lord,
    the Maker of heaven and earth.

Psalm 115:11, 14-15

I know that when the stress has grown too strong, you will be there.
I know that when the waiting seems so long, you hear my prayer.
I know that through the crash of falling worlds you're holding me.
I know that life and death are yours eternally.

— Mother Jane Stuart

Soul Writing

Write about a situation in your life — maybe something that happened recently — that seemed very bad but turned out positively in some way. Were you surprised? What did you learn? If such a thing happened again, would you think about it differently?

24
A Clump of Grass, a Corkscrew — Signs of Peace

Something to Think About

Brian Cavanaugh tells a story about a missionary who made regular monthly trips to a small South Pacific island. There he would do ordinary pastoral work: celebrate Mass, baptize children, witness marriage vows, anoint the sick, and pray for the recently deceased. The people in one particular village practiced a custom whenever the priest landed in his seaplane.

The village chief was always the first to greet the padre when he landed. They would hug; then the chief gave a clump of grass to the priest. The priest blessed the clump, gave it back to the chief, who in turn gave it to whoever is standing next to him, who gave it to the person next to him, who gave it to the next, until everyone in the village has passed it. Finally, the clump of grass comes back to the priest.

It's been years. The corkscrew is still in the front of the drawer. It reminds me to give in every now and then. Not take myself so seriously. Not allow conflict to reach a ridiculous point.

The clump goes through household after household. According to island custom, the chunk of earth with its tuft of grass is a sacred reminder of God's presence to these people who live in isolation on their island. They consider the clump a symbol of unity and peace, especially important to people forced into close community. The clump of grass tells all the others that you are in unity with them. There is no anger or resentment or hatred between you, your family, neighbors, God.

The ritual is complete when the clump is back in the hands of the priest, and at this point Mass can begin — not before.

On one visit, the priest blessed the clump, passed it to the leader, and began making preparations for Mass as the dirt made its way around the village. As the customary time for Mass approached, word came to the priest that there would be a delay.

There was a bitter disagreement between a father and son in one household, and the clump of earth had not been exchanged between them.

There was no celebration of Mass that month. Or the next. Or the next. It took a full three months before peace was restored to that family and to the island village.

Making It Mine

He had moved the corkscrew again. My husband and I were locked in our own battle over a "clump of earth." Only this conflict centered on a corkscrew.

We have a drawer in our kitchen where silverware and other small utensils are kept: spatulas, bottle opener, paring knives, potato peeler … corkscrew. It's my habit to pull the silverware tray to the front of the drawer and put the corkscrew in back. I've been doing it that way for years.

My new husband did just the opposite, push the tray back, place the corkscrew in the front of the drawer.

When I first noticed the misplacement of the corkscrew, I simply moved it without much thought. Until it kept happening — almost daily. After a little while it became a battle of wills. What right did he have moving the corkscrew anyway? It's not like he knows his way around the kitchen, and he doesn't even like wine. It became a kind of silent judgment on my ability to organize and think through problems. Did he think I wasn't capable of such a simple task?

Not that he had ever said such a thing. No. He simply moved the stupid corkscrew every chance he had. Annoying.

We never talked about this. He pushed the tray back, I pulled it forward. Over and over … until the day I opened the drawer, saw it there in the wrong place, and took a deep breath.

How much time and energy had I given that corkscrew anyway? In that instant it became the sign of our unity as a couple. In our home, love is the rule and we compromise and give ourselves to other people — unless you happen to misplace the corkscrew.

That day I left the corkscrew where it was. I shut the drawer and walked away with the peace of mind that comes from not having to be right and not having to prove anything.

I think I know how that South Pacific father and son must have felt when the clump of dirt passed from one hand to another. I accepted my husband's right to do something different than I might. It was like taking the clump of grass from his hands and letting peace fill the space between us.

It's been years. The corkscrew is still in the front of the drawer. It reminds me to give in every now and then. Not take myself so seriously. Not allow conflict to reach a ridiculous point. It reminds me to allow the people I love enough room to disagree with me.

A clump of dirt and grass can become a sacred symbol of unity. So can a corkscrew. In some houses a phone might be just such a symbol — especially if people are fighting over it. Maybe car keys, bath towels left on the floor … whatever object represents the conflict can represent unity too. It tells that conflict can be transformed into peace with a little effort.

What would happen in families and churches if just such a sacred sign were passed around before Eucharist? Well … it is. That's what we do when we speak words of peace and shake hands or hug or smile at the people around us just before receiving Eucharist. Think about your hands as holding the sacred chunk of grass and passing it off to those around you. Or … if it works better, think about holding a corkscrew.

 ## Prayer Starter

Come, let us bow down in worship,
   let us kneel before the Lord our Maker;
for he is our God
   and we are the people of his pasture,
   the flock under his care.
Today, if you hear his voice,
   do not harden your hearts.

Psalm 95:6-8a

God of us all, you have called us to be a family. We belong to one another, but somehow we often remain divided and indifferent. Never let me be content to dismiss others or leave conflict unresolved. Keep me restless to grow in love and peace.

Soul Writing

Write about conflict in your life. How do you handle it? What action could you take to resolve a conflict? How might you take the Christian call to be a peacemaker more seriously?

25
Keep Your Eyes Open
(You Might See Someone's Soul)

Something to Think About

A father discovers "windows of the soul," glimpses, he says, "of some of the things that are dear to God."

My daughter asked if I would take her to see a friend who was playing in a roller hockey game. The friend was a boy whom I'll call Joey. He had cerebral palsy, my daughter said, and he had asked her at school Friday if she would come and watch him play....

When we arrived at the roller rink, I went in with her thinking I could find a quiet nook and get some work done.... I was looking for an out-of-the-way place to write when my daughter pointed out Joey. He was playing goalie, hidden behind shin guards, face mask, and a chest guard.... All I noticed was that he stood a foot taller and years older than the other players.

Gathered at the railing behind Joey were four boys from my daughter's school. She joined them while I nested in a vacant table.... But the sight of those five high-school kids and the sound of their cheering distracted me. I stopped and paused and wondered if there was something I should be paying attention to, something that might prove to be a window of the soul.... I watched. I listened....

"Way to go, Joey," one of the boys calls out.

The other team scores against him.

"It's all right, Joey."

Joey blocks a shot.

The five high-school kids cheer, "Way to go, Joey."

The game goes back and forth from the far goal to the near one. Joey shows dissatisfaction with the way he's playing.

"Don't worry, Joey."

The four boys sit clumped on a round table. My daughter is off to the side. Joey makes another save, and all of them cheer. My daughter finally gets tired of standing and sits on the table with the boys.

"Way to hustle. Great defense. Yeah."

"Good job, Joey."

One by one they get up and lean on the railing, closer to the action. Joey pounds the floor with his hockey stick.

"Joey, you're doing great."

From *Windows of the Soul* by Ken Gire

Something glorious

in Gire's daughter

and those young

men enabled them

to transcend the

way most of us

react most of the

time and to cheer

their hearts out

for Joey.

Making It Mine

I like Gire's idea about windows of the soul. Windows that we peek through to see things more clearly, see them for the holiness present to us in that special moment in time we're living just now.

Familiarity makes us think we know already what we're looking at and so we don't really see the thing. What Gire saw between those five high-schoolers and goalie Joey was indeed a sacred moment. Joey was one of them. He wasn't trapped in isolation by his difference.

Something glorious in Gire's daughter and those young men enabled them to transcend the way most of us react most of the time and to cheer their hearts out for Joey. This isn't what usually happens; we all know it. But dreaming the possibility chokes us up, doesn't it? We've touched and been touched by the heart of God.

Patricia Livingston, author, tells a story of being in line in a grocery store when the black woman in front of her turns around and asks, "Did you get eggs? They're on special."

"No, I didn't see them."

"Well, girl, you got to keep your eyes open."

You'll see amazing things if you keep your eyes open.

Prayer Starter

How can a young man keep his way pure?
    By living according to your word.
I seek you with all my heart;
    do not let me stray from your commands.

Psalm 119:9-10

God, open my eyes and open my heart. Help me watch for windows to the soul of life, windows onto your holiness in those around me.

 # Soul Writing

Reflect on what has happened today and in the last few days. Did you see someone doing something good? Was there a moment, or moments, when your mind turned to thoughts of God? When did you feel strongly loved?

26
"What'cha Gonna Do About That?"

Something to Think About

A young man has had an intense experience of God's presence. The story continues. (See page 111 about reading Sessions 26-28 consecutively.)

Somehow Jason knew not to speak to anyone about what had happened.... Jason knew he had been singled out — for what, he didn't know except that it was important. It was not until the middle of his freshman year in college that Jason felt he needed to do anything.... The weekend before, he had gone with a friend to a downtown soup kitchen and helped feed the five hundred men, women, and children who shuffled through. It really shook him, watching their faces and thinking about the contrast between their life and his own....

We search aimlessly when we search for our call, our vocation. We will not find it — it will find us. It is a response from our deepest true self. It is a coming into the right place.

Jason's parents were dismayed at his decision to drop out of college and live in the inner city with the kitchen workers. The building the team lived in had no heat and no hot water, and they ate the discarded supermarket spoils along with those in the soup lines. Jason earned the grand sum of ten dollars a month.... They shared a daily Eucharist and weekly Bible study.... After a few months Jason even started a vegetable garden....

At the end of the first year, Jason signed up for another year despite the protests of his parents and grandparents, who feared he wouldn't "amount to anything" without a college education. He was realistic about the dangers of life in the inner city.... He had lived in the community long enough to know that there were severe personality problems even among those committed to serving the poor.... But he was living day by day — the way he knew he had to.

[The writer reflects:]

God's call in me reveals itself through my own yearning to become something I cannot quite name nor can I quite hide. My deep inner desire or gladness is the guide to God's will for me, and when I have moved deeper than the surface distractions that distort my true inner desire, then indeed I can trust it and follow it joyfully.

From *Friend of the Soul: A Benedictine Spirituality of Work*
by Norvene Vest

Making It Mine

Jason has learned something crucial. We search aimlessly when we search for our call, our vocation. We will not find it — it will find us. Vocation is found in the thing we can't escape doing because it's so much a part of who we are. It is a response from our deepest true self. It is a coming into the right place.

Norvene Vest writes about the Benedictine vision of work. The monks understand work as sacrament. Work as a high calling. Work as splendidly ordinary and holy. Work does not call us away from something. It calls us to *Someone*.

Randy Stonehill, one of the first to record what is usually called contemporary Christian music, wrote an early song about falling in love and sensing a call to that person — a call to a shared life, a sense that he's heading home. He ends the song with the challenge, "What'cha gonna do about that?"

Vocation can be recognized because that's the question it poses. What will you do with who you are — how will you live the Gospel in times like these?

"What'cha gonna do about that?"

Prayer Starter

The unfolding of your words gives light;
   it gives understanding to the simple.
Direct my footsteps according to your word;
   let no sin rule over me.

Psalm 119:130, 133

Father, Son, Holy Spirit. You are my God, the God of my life and my decisions. Light up my path, be my path, as I seek your will for me and listen for your call. I reach for the stars.

Soul Writing

Spend some time writing about your dreams and your longings for your life. What are your strengths? What do others say about your gifts? What makes you happiest? What experience of work or service has been significant for you? Do you hear a call? What does all this tell you about possible vocations?

27
Thy Kingdom Come

Something to Think About

Our Father, who art in heaven, hallowed be Thy name.
Thy kingdom come;
Thy will be done on earth as it is in heaven.
Give us this day our daily bread;
and forgive us our trespasses as we forgive those who
    trespass against us;
and lead us not into temptation,
but deliver us from evil.
Amen.

Making It Mine

This is probably the most familiar prayer you know. You probably know it so well that you haven't read it or seen it on a page in a very long time. It's put to mind so you don't need to read it.

Before you read any farther, go back. Read the Our Father again. Read it slowly. Then come back to this place.

I had a memorable week-long Benedictine experience near my home in Michigan with Father Dan Homan — the man whose warm, friendly face you see on the book jacket — and his longtime partner in retreat ministry, Mary Cummings. For many years they've held an event called Project People. The idea: get a group of young people and a few adults together to live in community at the monastery for a week. Ask them to pray daily — and to work in the service of others until they drop.

That's how I came to be standing in the white-hot parking lot of a refugee center in downtown Detroit praying the Our Father on a July day with a circle of teenagers. A few minutes later we would be inside the building painting walls, meeting people, and playing with kids. I had never prayed in a parking lot before. It changed forever how I will pray that prayer.

We dared to pray "Thy kingdom come" in one of our country's most troubled cities where there's very little evidence of a coming kingdom. We prayed it in a place where people have fled for their lives (the refugee center) from the kingdoms of tyrants and bullies and dictators. When we prayed "Thy kingdom come," it felt like an act of

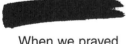

When we prayed "Thy kingdom come," it felt like an act of rebellion.

rebellion against all evil that had forced these people from the four corners of the earth to a small spot of earth where the air was too hot to breathe. Yet we stood there and said right out loud, "Thy kingdom come."

We prayed "give us this day our daily bread" and we sat down on church steps and ate our peanut-butter-and-jelly sandwiches. That was our lunch every day. The bread was better after the work. The kids said things like, "Wow, this is the best sandwich I've ever had." Sure, we'd eventually go back to our comfortable homes, manicured lawns, and full freezers, but that day we were part of those who relied on God for their daily bread. We felt genuine gratitude for each bite. Give us this day our daily peanut butter.

One afternoon I spent scrubbing the hallway rug after our workers had trampled all over it with paint on their sneakers and sandals. White footprints up the hallway and around the corner. "Forgive us our trespasses" kept ringing in my head.

We leave our footprints everywhere. We trespass irreverently, even selfishly. We violate and we go where we have no business going. God is wiping up the mess, scrub brush in hand. Forgive us our trespasses.

As we work, we meet people. There's an old man on the third floor who can never go home again. He weeps when he talks about it. He'll die among strangers.

Deliver us from evil. Please.

The day's work is over. We clean our brushes, say good-bye to our new friends, and go outside where the temperature is still 95 degrees in the shade. We circle up while holding hands. We're holding each other up. We have the nerve, after all we've seen, to do it again. We pray "Thy kingdom come" and we mean it.

Thy kingdom come is our way of life for that week. But maybe, if we've really prayed, really worked, really paid attention and listened, we'll make what we're praying a way of life — on earth as it is in heaven. Amen.

Prayer Starter

Defend the cause of the weak and fatherless;
    maintain the rights of the poor and oppressed.
Rescue the weak and needy;
    deliver them from the hand of the wicked.
Psalm 82:3-4

Father, I do not know your ways. I cannot know how you answer prayer, or how you heal the land, or how you will bring your kingdom. I know that something is very wrong around me. But I believe you do *answer prayer and you* are *healing my world and you are healing me and a kingdom* is *coming. Thy kingdom come.*

Soul Writing

Go through the Lord's prayer line by line, word by word, and write about how each phrase impacts your own life and the world you experience daily.

28
Between a Rock and a Hard Case

Something to Think About

Try to read Sessions 26-28 consecutively, not all at the same time, but in three consecutive readings. The background for the experience described in this session is found in Session 27.

Below the surface something like rage was building up in me, ready to surge outward. I got ready to verbally pulverize her as soon as she took a breath in her angry monologue. As I started to open my mouth and let loose, my hand brushed the red rag at my waist. I suddenly remembered.

Friday, the final work day of Project People. The monastery van was filled with teens, our work supplies, and the cooler with our peanut-butter-and-jelly sandwiches. We were in good spirits all morning as my crew looked forward to working on an outside project rather than being inside in the sweltering heat.

I walked out of the retreat house with a couple of the boys toward the van where my crew gathered. Across the yard Brother Damien, one of the monks, was walking with his crew; he waved at us and smiled. "Have a great day!" he shouted.

"You too!" I replied and waved back.

Then he hesitated. I saw wheels turning behind those big brown eyes. He motioned me over. "Come here, my friend, I want to talk to you," he called. I walked over to him and he wrapped his very long arms around me in a warm hug, then pulled a red rag seemingly out of nowhere, and pushed it into my hand.

"Here. You need this," he said. I glanced at the clean painter's rag, tucked it into my waistband, kissed his bearded cheek, and was off for the day.

At the work site, we faced a crisis. Because of miscommunication, my crew was expected to undo some of the work previously accomplished. A very hostile staff member of the agency explained all this. She was cold, angry, complaining, and demanding. The people who worked for her — and the kids on my crew — were visibly shaken. I started to fume. Something inside me was ready to boil over. She was unreasonable. She was ungrateful. She was completely self-focused. She was saying things I knew were not true. She was a bully.

It had been a great week. We had new friends in these displaced people. The children and the teens loved one another instantly. The staff liked and trusted us. We had accomplished more than anyone could have dreamed. All the good seemed to be crumbling before my eyes in the last hours. Below the surface something like rage was building up in me, ready to surge outward. I got ready to verbally pulverize her as soon as she took a breath in her angry monologue. As

I started to open my mouth and let loose, my hand brushed the red rag at my waist. I suddenly remembered.

I remembered who I am. I remembered who we were, and what we were representing, and that our mission was to serve, not to be right or prove anything. We had prayed only moments before, "… as we forgive those who trespass against us."

If she wanted the whole place unpainted, our mission for the day would be unpainting. I agreed to do as she expected. When she exited the site, a staff member helped us with the work and we were done in no time. We were home at the monastery by lunch.

 ## Making It Mine

There's a rock in my office that was given to me by a dying girl on a beach a little north of home. It is a symbol that reminds me to celebrate life. The red rag Brother Damien gave me is a symbol that reminds me to think before ripping into another human being.

A man who shares the office building with me carries a rosary in his pocket. He's not the kind of guy you'd expect to have a rosary in his pocket. But he's trying to remember that his spirituality is important. My husband wears a pewter cross on a chain around his neck. It reminds him of what matters most.

I've heard people talk about how boring church is. "It's the same thing over and over," they say. If that's true, it's because we are not engaging our minds, hearts, and spirits. It isn't the fault of the ritual or tradition. It's our problem.

Ritual, repetition, and tradition cause something important to be carved on our hearts, increasing the chances of our remembering. Symbols gather up great depth of meaning and significance into something we can hold in our hand. The Communion cup, the sign of the cross, holy water, candles in the dark.…

But we have to connect to the symbol or it's empty for us, personally. To connect, we must be paying attention.

Prayer Starter

Teach me, O Lord, to follow your decrees;
    then I will keep them to the end.
Give me understanding, and I will keep your law
    and obey it with all my heart.
Turn my heart toward your statutes
    and not toward selfish gain.
Turn my eyes away from worthless things.

Psalm 119:33-34, 36-37a

God be in my head and in my understanding;
God be in my eyes, and in my looking;
God be in my mouth, and in my speaking;
God be in my heart, and in my thinking.

— *The Sarum Primer (1558)*

 **Soul Writing**

Write about your "traditions." What symbols do you wear or keep that are reminders of something important? Do you have keepsakes from friends? Something that reminds you of a great vacation or a trip you really liked? Does your family have traditions? Include religious traditions.

29
What Makes Catholics Different?

Something to Think About

A Catholic writer finds something distinctive about Catholics.

Catholics believe, quietly and in all humility, that Catholicism carries the deepest potential for Christian joy.... Catholic joy comes, in part, from being able to relate to the Divine Mystery through an almost embarrassing wealth of metaphors, all of which are true, none of which ever say it all.... Evelyn Waugh, a twentieth-century English Catholic, wrote a now familiar verse:

Where (ever) the Catholic sun does shine
There's music and laughter and good red wine.

... As Catholic singer and songwriter John Stewart wrote, "... You can survive the darkest night/Remembering the sun...."

From *The Joy of Being Catholic* by Mitch Finley

Making It Mine

The primary historical difference between Catholics and Protestants isn't ethics or theology. We agree on more than we disagree. The fundamental, traditional difference has to do with how we see the world. We call this our worldview. Whenever we start talking about worldviews, the risk of painting one group with broad strokes is possible. Worldviews vary, even within a group we define by a singular label like "Protestant."

This "Catholic distinctive" calls us to celebrate our lives, to love fiercely, to pursue justice, and to believe that we are capable of more good than we've ever dreamed and more love than we've ever known.

Worldview is the set of preconceptions through which we filter all information. Everyone has preconceptions. These are so deeply imbedded in who we are that some psychologists have called them preconscious.

Of course, the worldviews of Catholics and Protestants aren't completely different — only somewhat different, but different enough to influence how we "do" life. Researchers have shown us that Protestants tend to view God as radically absent from the world because the world is in the grip of sin, it is fallen. So, in the fallen world, God only occasionally is revealed. The world and all its objects are viewed as distinctly separate from God. Because of this, stronger lines are drawn between the secular and the sacred.

Catholics generally have what has been referred to as a "sacramental" mind. We believe God is present in all of creation, more present than we know how to grasp. The ordinary becomes holy. Human society is not "God-forsaken" but ordered of God, natural and good. People are good. Creation is good. The universe is friendly. This "Catholic distinctive" calls us to celebrate our lives, to love fiercely, to pursue justice, and to believe that we are capable of more good than we've ever dreamed and more love than we've ever known. It is thick with optimism and joy.

We celebrate this reality in Mass when the Divine dances among us, symbols of our earth and life and work are transformed, and we call down the fire to give us new life. In this we see the remarkable potential of the ordinary stuff of human life to become holy. When genuinely integrated into our everyday lives, we approach others reverently and we cease the endless consuming. We celebrate life instead. That is Catholic joy.

Prayer Starter

All the earth bows down to you;
    they sing praise to you,
    they sing praise to your name.
Praise our God, O peoples,
    let the sound of his praise be heard;
he has preserved our lives
    and kept our feet from slipping.

                                                    Psalm 66:4, 8-9

I thank you, God, for the pleasures you have given me through my senses, for the glory of thunder, for the mystery of music, the laughter of children. I thank you for the delight of color, the awe of the sunset, the wild roses, the smile of friendship. I thank you for the relentless sweetness. Truly, O Lord, the earth is full of your presence.

Soul Writing

Does it surprise you that Protestants and Catholics might see the world differently? Do you and your Protestant friends differ this way? Apart from the Catholic things you do — go to Church, youth group, etc. — do you *think* as a Catholic? Write about these questions.

30
Kleenex Company

Something to Think About

A pastor describes one of his most painful jobs.

I've had the privilege and pain of sitting with families in anguish over the death of a loved one. I have often witnessed the unlikely marriage of tears and laughter. We'll be seated in the living room, say, planning Bill's funeral. The silence of sorrow surrounds each sentence. "Why did he have to die so young?" Sharon says. "With two little children, with so much of a future ahead...." And maybe I mutter something ... or maybe I just cry with her.

Then George, who has just flown in from Denver to be with his sister, after a blast from his nose that might very well have raised Bill himself from the mortician's table, says, "If I'd known there were this many tears in the world, I'd have bought stock in the damn Kleenex company."

Silence follows, for about two seconds; no one's too sure how to respond, given the circumstances.... But then a snicker from one of the kids. It's enough. Like bubbles rising from the bottom of a kettle sitting long over the fire, the laughter rises to the surface until the whole room boils over with mirth far out of proportion to the humor in the comment.

A release of tension of course ... but more.... Sharon's eyes: she's looking at her big brother — the boy who had tried to force-feed a lizard down her throat as she screamed, the teenager who had begged for her help when he was going down for the third time in the sea of algebra, the college student who telephoned (collect) once a week for no reason other than he missed her, and the young man who had cried like a baby at her wedding — her big brother who wishes he'd bought stock in the damn Kleenex company, her big brother whom she loves with an ache almost as great as the ache in her heart because of her husband's death....

From *Finding Happiness in the Most Unlikely Places*
by Donald McCullough

The family is the community you will share all your life with. They will still be here in thirty years and they will know your whole story and they will love you anyway.

118

Making It Mine

Yvonne and Crystal are sisters. Crystal is two years older. As children, Crystal felt protective of her "little" sister, but as they entered their teen years a certain rivalry wedged itself between them, making those years a continual battleground. People who knew both young women had heard each of them say with conviction, "I hate my sister."

Turn the page. Both girls are now women in their twenties. One is a political and religious conservative; the other hasn't had a conservative thought since she was six. They wouldn't have chosen each other as friends, but they are sisters. A family is given to us; we don't pick one out for ourselves.

Maybe that's why the bond goes so deep and is almost unbreakable.

Not very long ago, Crystal's husband walked away from their short marriage of a few years. It plunged Crystal into a deep depression, the first despair she had ever known. She bottled up her emotions and became angry, unreachable.

Until the moment her baby sister Yvonne intruded into her life. She demanded that Crystal "start talking to me!" The big sister was cradled in the arms of her baby sister where she was free to sob and scream and swear and pray out loud until the rage ebbed away.

Friends, lovers, acquaintances — these people come and go. The family is the community you will share all your life with. They will still be here in thirty years and they will know your whole story and they will love you anyway. The family is a tiny replica of the whole race, the larger community. For better or worse we live out the story of the human race within our families. We learn how to love, forgive, tolerate, overlook, confront. All the sacred mysteries are enacted over and over within the borders, the confines, of the family. Some of us learn how to hate in our families. Some of us learn how to love. All of us learn how to live.

 # Prayer Starter

Be not far from me, O God;
   come quickly, O my God, to help me.
Though you have made me see troubles, many and bitter,
   you will restore my life again;
from the depths of the earth
   you will again bring me up
   and comfort me once again.

Psalm 71:12, 20-21b

Father, being part of a family seems, at various times, to be both a great trouble and an enfolding comfort. Open my heart to the lessons my family has to teach me — even the hard ones.

Soul Writing

Write about how it feels to be part of your family. What can you learn from what is going on in your family right now?

31
Change: Messy, Inevitable, Delightful

Something to Think About

In Lewis Carroll's *Through the Looking Glass,* that great children's story for adults, Alice has a confusing moment in her journey through Wonderland. She discovers that she isn't saying what she means to say. She is changing moment to moment. She feels at a loss to understand what is happening except that nothing is the same as it used to be. She wonders if anything will ever return to "normal."

… The Gryphon added, "Come, let's hear some of your adventures."

"I could tell you my adventures — beginning from this morning," said Alice a little timidly; "but it's no use going back to yesterday, because I was a different person then."

Making It Mine

Someone said that opinions are like clothing: as you grow they no longer fit you. In *Alice's Adventures in Wonderland,* the heroine discovers that the person she was isn't the person she is now. She is changing and she is helpless to stop the changing. That's what growing up and growing as a person is all about.

During high school, my brother and I shared a "best friend." His name was Don. Don's father committed suicide when Don was eleven. He came home from school and found him. That day, Don made himself a promise that he would never talk to God again. He told himself God wasn't real and God didn't care. End of story.

Except — Don is one of those very intelligent, analytical types who knows that 2 plus 2 must always equal 4. In college, as he studied to be a math teacher, he said he kept running into God like a "solid wall" he couldn't get past.

When I decided God wasn't real or wasn't the kind of God who merited my allegiance, that was that. Admitting I was wrong was really hard.

"My convictions are strong ones," he told me. "I don't hold wishy-washy opinions; so when I decided God wasn't real or wasn't the kind of God who merited my allegiance, that was that. Admitting I was wrong was really hard. I had announced my decision to so many people. But I kept seeing that the perfect order of all that exists which we can comprehend, and much that exists which we can't comprehend, called for an Originator, a Source bigger than us. It couldn't be escaped."

Change is not the enemy, even though it often brings complications with it. Change is inevitable. It brings us gifts of new insight, maturity, increased understanding when we open ourselves to the possibilities inherent in change.

Prayer Starter

I will listen to what God the Lord will say;
   he promises peace to his people.
Love and faithfulness meet together;
   righteousness and peace kiss each other.
Faithfulness springs forth from the earth,
The Lord will indeed give what is good.

Psalm 85:8a, 10, 11a, 12a

God, here I am.
You alone know fully why.
May I rest on that knowledge,
and let it bear me where you will.

 **Soul Writing**

Write about the ways your opinions and convictions are changing. How does change excite you? How does it threaten and discourage you? What changes have you noticed during the time you have been keeping this prayer journal?

32
For My Friend – A Pillow in the Gut

Something to Think About

Do you think monks are serious, sober, and shy? Kathleen Norris knows one who seemed so but wasn't.

One memorable evening I witnessed an inspired union of playfulness and thoughtful interpretation of Benedictine hospitality in the form of a vigorous pillow fight. I was visiting an abbey with a ten-year-old girl whose parents' divorce was becoming final in the next week. She and her mother had had a rough year, and the girl was getting her first taste of joint custody, spending the summer with her father. I met her at the bus stop that morning with a monk who carried a small bouquet; he'd picked some of the summer's last roses for the girl, because her name was Rose.

I can't count the times when a friend who is already overworked, overcommitted, and downright tired has set aside his or her own pressing concerns to listen and be present to me.

The pressures on this child were considerable; among other things, she feared the possibility of having to testify in a custody hearing. I was grateful to be able to offer her a day of play; we called on the abbot, walked the abbey grounds, pulled a few weeds in a flower bed, and attended a ceremony at which a novice received his monastic name, a solemn form of play that fascinated the girl.

One young monk, extremely introverted, befriended her at lunch and came to our room after Vespers. But she had become tired and whiny, and fell on her bed with exaggerated drama, clutching a pillow. As the monk got up to leave, he carried off a move that would have done Buster Keaton proud, snatching the pillow from under her head and whacking her with it. Taken by surprise, Rose was both affronted and delighted. She grabbed another pillow, stood on the bed, and hit him back — and the fight was on. It continued for nearly a half hour and was marked by brilliant tactics on both sides. When the girl grabbed the monk by his scapular, he pointed out that she had merely drawn him closer, making it easier for him to hit her. She groaned and deposited one more blow to his head. He got her in the stomach.

When the two had finally had enough (I became exhausted just watching them), the monk left and we went to bed. Rose slept soundly for fourteen hours. And that was the point: to give a frightened little girl a chance to hit — and hit hard — tiring her so she couldn't help but have a good night's sleep. All she had to do was be herself, a little girl who enjoys a pillow fight. In putting the child's needs before his own, the monk was doing battle with his natural shyness. He was also having fun. It was Benedictine hospitality at its best.

From *Dakota: A Spiritual Geography* by Kathleen Norris

Making It Mine

I once heard hospitality described as "making room for others in your life." What that means to me is that hospitality is about friendship. In friendship, we make a place for someone else to share our life. It means moving past ourselves, just as the young monk in the story did. Out of concern and care for the little girl he stretched himself beyond his own introversion and did what didn't come naturally.

Most of us have someone who does the same for us. I can't count the times when a friend who is already overworked, overcommitted, and downright tired has set aside his or her own pressing concerns to listen and be present to me. Friendship involves a commitment to do exactly that.

Songwriter and musician Charlie Peacock writes of a man who wakes up deeply troubled in the middle of the night and discovers there is no one with whom he can confidently "dare disturb the sleep of friends." Whenever I hear this song, it brings to mind the people I could call if I had such a night. I hope too that they know they can call me on a night like that. I hope they know that if it's a pillow fight they need, it's a pillow fight they'll get. And if I discover they need to "hit hard," maybe I can have the courage to take the blows.

Prayer Starter

Unless the Lord builds the house,
　its builders labor in vain.

Psalm 127:1

Father, you are my Father. You are the Father of my friends and family too. Teach me to be faithful to the ones I love and to make room for them in my life. Bring us together in a house of love and friendship that you build.

Soul Writing

Have you ever needed someone to listen to you and couldn't find anyone to "make room" for you? How did it feel? Are you making room for others in your life? Write about a few practical ways you could be more loving and open in your relationships with both friends and family.

33
Bars of Hope

Something to Think About

An American notices something about Mexico.

Driving through the streets of Mexico City one day, I was intrigued by the large number of homes that had long metal bars rising up above their roofs.

Looking over the city, there are thousands of buildings large and small that have steel bars rising above them. I asked the driver to explain the metal sticking up from the homes. He said they are called *barras de esperanza*, which translates, "bars of hope."

"When families build their homes, " he said, "they often don't have the money or resources to complete the project. Perhaps they don't know how large of a family they will have. So they take what they have and begin the project. When they have completed as much as possible, they leave the structural bars rising above the home as a visible symbol for their neighbors and anyone who happens to pass by the house, saying, 'We are not finished with this house, yet.' These are bars of hope to remind us that we are still building, to demonstrate that there is more to come."

From *Coloring Outside the Lines* by John Westfall

There will be another concert, and another song. Another day for building is sure to arrive. Your chance will come around again.

Making It Mine

John Michael Talbot, musician and monk, walked to the center of the stage, guitar in hand. Those of us in the small audience for this private performance looked at one another a bit perplexed. How would he sing? He hardly looked able to stand.

Talbot was pale, shaky, moving very slowly, with sweat forming droplets along his hairline. He didn't have to tell us he was sick. We knew.

He explained that he very much wanted to sing for us. "But I don't know if I can," he admitted. "So I'm going to sing until I can't anymore."

Fair enough, we thought. Can't ask anyone for more than that.

That's what he did, he sang. Three songs. He sang two songs to us. On the third he did something unexpected, he asked us to help him sing it. The simple first line was, "Let nothing trouble you…." He sang it. We sang it back. He stopped strumming his guitar. We stopped singing.

"You're making all the clichés about Catholic singing true," he grinned. We laughed lowly. "I know you can do better." Just sitting upright was obviously difficult for him. He was going downhill as he struggled to continue. Well, okay, we'll try again, the audience seemed to respond. We inhaled deeply, simultaneously — and the next time it was our turn to sing, we let it rip.

And we were rewarded with a bright Talbot smile as he said softly, "Ah … beautiful. Very nice. You did great.…" His every word and movement drained him more. He was even paler and growing weaker. Everyone suspected food poisoning of some sort.

He held his guitar for just a moment and looked like he wanted to play, then set it aside and rose. "I apologize, but I can't go on," he said in a whispery voice. He was helped off stage. We would hear later that he recovered and was well.

He left his guitar propped against the stage's edge that night. The symbol of his best intention to finish. Maybe he had even hoped to come back that same night, I don't know. But when we left the room the guitar was still there. A strange sort of icon of hope.

We get sidetracked. We need help. We've done all we can. There is a time to admit that you can't go on. There's no shame in that, you know. And that's not the last word either.

There will be another concert, and another song. Another day for building is sure to arrive. Your chance will come around again. Every dead end comes with its own "bars of hope." These are the small bits of evidence scattered along your path that what is started will be finished — someday.

It's a bar of hope we leave for all the world to see when we pray, "… Thy kingdom come." It has come among us … and is still coming among us … and isn't finished coming among us. Look for the bars of hope.

Prayer Starter

Save me, O God,
>   for the waters have come up to my neck.
I am worn out calling for help;
>   my throat is parched.
My eyes fail,
>   looking for my God.

Psalm 69:1, 3

Dear God, sometimes it's hard to keep putting one foot in front of another. What's the use? Even my best efforts sometimes come out all wrong or come to a screeching halt and I can't do anything about it. Give me sight of the bars of hope.

Soul Writing

What are you now discouraged about or have been discouraged about? What bars of hope are in this situation? What can you do to be ready when the second chance comes around?

34
When You're Out of Kisses, Say So

Something to Think About

When my two daughters were toddlers we had a routine. They would come to me just before going to bed every night for a slobbery good-night kiss and a story. Sometimes I would kind of slump in the chair, look forlornly pathetic, and announce that it had been a difficult day and Mommy was all out of kisses. So they'd have to give me a bunch of them and fill up my supply. Childish and simple, but we enjoyed it.

When Andrea was three she went into the hospital with pneumonia and a temperature of 106. She really didn't know how to tell me, at that age, just how frightened she was. I sat at the edge of the huge metal crib all night long. Just before daybreak, she opened her wide, dark, green eyes and looked at me. She made a very sad face and said, "I'm outta kisses."

When Shelly had just finished her first week of first grade — school all day — she had learned the hard reality that sometimes she had to sit still, listen, and not talk. Never easy for her. Still isn't. I met her at the bus stop that Friday as usual. She climbed slowly down the steps and watched the bus pull away. She stooped over and pulled up her white knee-socks drooping around her ankles, then straightened up to her full height. Reaching for my hand to walk toward home she said with a shake of her head, "I'm really out of kisses, Mom."

Communicate your needs to the people you love. Tell them how you feel. Reach out for a hug when you need it. Say ouch when it hurts.

Making It Mine

My brother was a newlywed of only a few months. He'd stopped by my apartment after work early one evening for coffee. He described the previous evening with his bride. He had known this girl since they were sixteen. He wondered out loud, "How could you know someone five years and not see this side of them?"

"I knew she was mad at me," he said. "She just had that look. So I asked her, 'What's wrong?' She said, 'Nothing.' Okay. Half an hour later she still has the look. I ask again. 'Honey, I can tell you're upset. What's wrong?' 'Nothing,' she says. We go to bed. 'Darling, Baby, Sugar … what's wrong?' I plead. 'I told you,' she growls at me, 'nothing is wrong!' and rolls over. I don't get it. I go to sleep. This morning she announces that I'm an insensitive creep and storms out the door."

I poured his coffee, saying, "That's because you're a man, and an idiot, besides being an insensitive creep. You were supposed to keep asking. 'Nothing is wrong' means 'Ask me again.' "

He drank his coffee silently and looked even more baffled.

We all need comfort, support, and understanding. Sometimes we need these things badly. And we have a right to expect it from those who say they love us. Remember, though — they're only human. They don't read minds. Communicate your needs to the people you love. Tell them how you feel. Reach out for a hug when you need it. Say ouch when it hurts. Warn people when you're angry. It's going to get dark and it's going to get cold and you'll feel the cold in your bones sometimes. Tell someone. Let that person love you. Admit it when you're out of kisses.

 ## Prayer Starter

I said, "Oh, that I had the wings of a dove!
    I would fly away and be at rest —
I would hurry to my place of shelter,
    far from the tempest and storm."
Cast your cares on the Lord
    and he will sustain you.

Psalm 55:6, 8, 22a

Father, when I am so lost and hurt that I can't tell others of my pain or need, I know you see and care. But if I'm going to get love and give love in this world, I'll have to tell others about it. Give me the words. Give me the courage to speak.

Soul Writing

Write about a situation like the one my brother was in with his wife — a time when someone you cared about expected you to know, without being told, what he or she was thinking and wanting. Write about your feelings at the time, and your feelings when you finally realized what was happening.

35
He Was One of Us

Something to Think About

Carlo Carretto, a member of a religious order working in an impoverished country, tells about a stork that was wounded in one of the traps villagers set to capture food for their families.

They perceive me as a constant threat. To change their perceptions would require a form of incarnation.

All that night she lost blood…. All attempts to save the poor bird were useless: she died that same day and we buried her….

The flight of storks set out once more for the north, but the partner of the dead stork stayed behind. That evening we saw the wretched bird come down near the garden, in the same place that his partner had been trapped, and fly round and round, crying and showing obvious signs that he was looking for something. This went on until sunset. The same scene was repeated the next day…. He stayed for the entire year. Each day he would go off in search of food, and at sunset we would see his outline against the sky over the garden, as he came down in the usual place…. It was moving to see how sensitive this creature was to the love and attention of the brothers…. I remember the look in his eyes, his habit of cocking his head on one side, the regular movement of his beak, and the way he had of staring at me, as if he were trying to catch hold of me and escape from his solitude. I for my part tried to understand him, but I remained myself, and he remained a stork…. There was no possibility of communication.

From *Letters from the Desert* by Carlo Carretto

Making It Mine

In I Was Just Wondering, *author Philip Yancey writes about his aquarium.**

Even here, in the beauty of my artificial universe, suffering thrives as well…. The spikes and fins on my lion fish are appropriately menacing; they can contain enough toxin to kill a person. And when any one fish shows a sign of weakness, the others will turn on it, tormenting without mercy. Just last week the other six fish were brutally attacking the infected eye of the cowfish; in aquariums pacifists die young.

I spend much time and effort fighting off the parasites, bacteria, and fungi that invade the tank. I run a portable chemical laboratory to test the specific gravity, nitrate and nitrite levels, and ammonia content. I pump in vitamins and antibiotics and sulfa drugs, and enough enzymes to make a rock grow.... You would think, in view of all this energy expended on their behalf, that my fish would at least be grateful. Not so. Every time my shadow appears above the tank, they dive for cover into the nearest shell. Three times a day I open the lid and drop in food, yet they respond to each opening as a sure sign of my designs to torture them. Fish are not affirming pets.

The arduous demands of aquarium management have taught me a deep appreciation for what is involved in running a universe based on dependable physical laws. To my fish I am deity, and one who does not hesitate to intervene. I balance the salts and trace elements in their water. No food enters their tank unless I retrieve it from my freezer and drop it in. They would not live a day without the electrical gadget that brings oxygen to the water.

Whenever I must treat an infection, I face an agonizing choice. Ideally, I should move the infected fish to a quarantine tank in order to keep the others from pestering it and to protect them from contagion. But such violent intervention in the tank, the mere act of chasing the sick fish with the net, could do more damage than the infection.... I often long for a way to communicate with those small-brained water-dwellers. Out of ignorance, they perceive me as a constant threat. I cannot convince them of my true concern. I am too large for them, my actions too incomprehensible ... my acts of mercy they see as cruelty; my attempts at healing they view as destruction. To change their perceptions would require a form of incarnation.

*Excerpted from *I Was Just Wondering* by Philip Yancey, Wm. B. Eerdmans Publishing Co., copyright © 1989; used by permission

In what we Christians call the Incarnation, God becomes human — fully human. God joins us in the mess so that he can lead us out of it. Calvin Miller, in The Singer, *wrote it this way:*

Earthmaker set earth spinning
on its way
And said, "Give me your vast
infinity
My son; I'll wrap it in a bit
of clay
Then enter Terra microscop
ically
To love the little souls who
weep away
Their lives." "I will," I said,
"set Terra free."

 ## Prayer Starter

For this God is our God for ever and ever;
    he will be our guide even to the end.

                                Psalm 48:14

Lord Jesus Christ, in you God has come down to walk among us. I can't fully understand what that means. Help me to see you. Leap into my heart, as you have leapt into human life.

 **Soul Writing**

Think a bit on this question: what does it mean for you that God became one of us? A recent song asked, "What if God were one of us … just a stranger on a bus trying to make his way home?" What do you think of this image of God?

36
She Thinks I'm Real!

Something to Think About

We are all born with the right to human dignity and respect. No one should be denied this. But becoming human is also a gradual process.

A waitress was taking orders from a couple and their young son. She was one of the class of veteran waitresses who never show outright disrespect to their customers but who frequently make it quietly evident by their unhurried pace and their level stare that they fear no mortal, not even parents. She jotted on her pad deliberately and silently as the father and mother gave their selection and gratuitous instructions as to what was to be substituted for what, and which dressing changed to what sauce.

When she finally turned to the boy, he began his order with a kind of fearful desperation. "I want a hot dog —" he started. And both parents barked at once, "No hot dog!" The mother went on. "Bring him the lyonnaise potatoes and the beef, both vegetables, and a hard roll and —"

The waitress wasn't even listening. She said evenly to the youngster, "What do you want on your hot dog?" He flashed an amazed smile.

"Ketchup, lots of ketchup, and — bring a glass of milk."

"Coming up," she said as she turned from the table, leaving behind the stunned silence of utter parental dismay. The boy watched her go before he turned to his father and mother with astonished elation to say, "You know what? She thinks I'm real! She thinks I'm real!"

From "She Thinks I'm Real" from *Illustrations Unlimited*
by Frederick B. Speakman

Making It Mine

What makes a person real? Put another way, what about you or someone else is real enough to invoke respect and reverence? Seems like a strange question. The incredible state of being human, in itself, should be enough to invoke reverence. Every person is an idea of God's and a miracle waiting to be discovered and unleashed.

A song in the Disney version of *The Hunchback of Notre Dame* asked the question "Who is the monster and who is the man?" It's a familiar theme we've encountered in movies such as *The Elephant Man, Mask, Powder,* and *Rainman.*

Margery Williams's classic, *The Velveteen Rabbit*, tells the story of a new toy bunny that comes to live in a child's nursery. More than anything, the Rabbit wants to be "real." Skin Horse is an old, well-loved, favorite toy whom Rabbit turns to for advice. Skin Horse's advice is this:

"Real ... it's a thing that happens to you. When a child loves you for a long, long time ... you become Real." The Rabbit asks, "Does it hurt?"

"Sometimes," Skin Horse answers. "Generally by the time you are Real, most of your hair has been loved off, and your eyes drop out and you get loose joints and very shabby. But these things don't matter at all because once you are Real, you can't be ugly, except to people who don't understand."

We are all born with the right to human dignity and respect. No one should be denied this. But becoming human is also a gradual process. We are born with the substance of God throbbing inside us, but it takes a lifetime to become comfortable in our skins and to become the most authentically human we are capable of becoming. Christians believe that to become like Jesus is to become real.

Contrary to what our culture tells us, being human isn't about contributing to the Gross National Product. It isn't about what we manufacture or the salary we command, our address, or the skills we're so proud of. Each of us is born gloriously human and each of us spends a lifetime growing more real. A great many people seem not to understand what makes us real. Like Rabbit, the journey begins in the crib. One of the most important lessons we learn along the way is to revere one another. We are all real. We are all becoming more real.

 ## Prayer Starter

Your hands made me and formed me;
   give me understanding to learn your commands.
May your unfailing love be my comfort,
   according to your promise to your servant.
Though I am like a wineskin in the smoke,
   I do not forget your decrees.

Psalm 119:73, 76, 83

Stretch out my heart with your strength, as you stretch out the sky above the earth. Smooth out any wrinkles of hatred or resentment. Enlarge my soul that it may know more fully your truth.
— *Gilbert of Hoyland*

 **Soul Writing**

Remember a time when you felt someone wasn't taking you seriously and treated you as if you were not "real." Write about it. What beliefs, habits, ideas, behaviors could keep you from becoming more real?

37

We Learn from Some Pretty Unusual People

Something to Think About

It was a stunning reminder of what we all knew. We are to greet the "lesser" among us as Christ himself.

Maxie Dunnam tells the story of a boy named Philip. He was born with Down's syndrome — mentally retarded. Philip was a happy child, but as he grew he also grew more aware that he was different from other kids.

Philip went to Sunday school with nine other eight-year-olds. They were the normal kind of eight-year-olds who can't bear to have anything, or anyone, be different. And Philip was different. Everyone could see that Philip was different. He didn't look like the other children; he didn't talk like them. Even his crafts — things like those gold spray-painted noodle-covered pencil boxes — never looked exactly like the other kids'.

The teacher was a great guy who understood eight-year-olds. He knew they were a good group of kids, kids who cared about one another, even though they might have a way of saying so at the top of their voices while making faces and stomping feet and rolling eyes. The teacher knew too that Philip wasn't really part of the group. Philip, of course, had never chosen *not* to be part of the group. He just wasn't part of it, and that was that.

One year the teacher had a great idea for Easter Sunday. He took ten of those egg-shaped things panty hose come in and presented them to his class. He explained that they were going to go outside on the church grounds and look for things that represented Easter. They would put their treasures in the egg containers and bring them back to the classroom.

A little while later, he sat at the table with ten panty-hose containers in front of him and ten wiggling, excited eight-year-olds beaming at him. One by one he opened the containers. In one was a flower, and they appropriately oo-ed and aah-ed. Another had a butterfly and the girls said, "Beautiful …" because it's very hard for boys to say it. He opened another and found a rock and a boy said, "That's mine because I knew you'd all do flowers and leaves and butterflies and stuff like that so I wanted to be different. See, it sparkles and for me that's Easter."

The teacher opened the next one and there was nothing in it. The other children said, almost in unison as children will, "That's not fair; someone didn't do it."

Philip said, "I did, I did too. I did it...."

"Philip," one of the boys said, "don't you ever do anything right? There's nothing there."

"I did so do it right," Philip insisted. "I did it. It's empty — the tomb is empty!"

The class was silent. A very rich silence. From that day on, a new life began for Philip. Things were different in the class after that. The other kids took him in. He entered. He was released from the tomb of his difference.

Not long after that, Philip died. It had never been expected that he would live a normal life span. He was buried from the church where he attended Sunday school. The day of his funeral, nine eight-year-olds, with their teacher, marched right up the center aisle to the too-tiny casket at the front, not with flowers or greens to prettify death. They stormed up the aisle and laid on it a basket with ten empty panty-hose containers. They had learned something about Easter, but they had also learned something about themselves — and Philip. And none of them would ever be the same again.

Adapted from *Communicator's Commentary*, Philippians, pp. 296-297, by Maxie Dunnam

 Making It Mine

We learn from people we never expect to learn from. In my hometown there have been a pair long familiar to everyone, Ezra and Bob. Both have mental and emotional disabilities. They share an apartment in an independent living program. Ezra is quite a lot older than Bob, old enough to be his father and then some. They are always seen all over town together. Every church knows them because they aren't particular what brand of Christianity they belong to: they'll be in a Baptist church one week, Lutheran the next, then Catholic and Methodist ... you get the idea.

Once, at the soup kitchen where I was cooking, a particular youngster was demanding that the staff pick the onions out of his soup. In line behind him were Ezra and Bob. Growing annoyed with the child, the server snapped, "Just take your soup and stop acting like you have special rights."

Ezra turned to Bob and said rather loudly, "That just ain't the right way to talk to Jesus."

It was a stunning reminder of what we all knew. We are to greet the "lesser" among us as Christ himself. It's been said by great spiritual writers and expounded upon by renowned scholars, but none had ever said it more effectively than Ezra.

Prayer Starter

But you, O God, do see trouble and grief;
   you consider it to take it in hand.
The victim commits himself to you;
   you are the helper of the fatherless.
Break the arm of the wicked and evil man;
   call him to account for his wickedness
   that would not be found out.
You hear, O Lord, the desire of the afflicted;
   you encourage them, and you listen to their cry,
defending the fatherless and the oppressed,
   in order that man, who is of the earth, may terrify no more.

Psalm 10:14-15, 17

Father, free me from my tomb of indifference and teach me to respect and honor all, even those who are very different. When I shun those who are different, it increases darkness in the world. I am part of the human community, and we are all woven together.

 Soul Writing

Think of someone you know who is ignored by others — someone who is out of it. Imagine what this person would feel like. Now imagine reaching out to this person and learning something from him or her. Write about that.

38
Something We Don't Like to Think About

Something to Think About

A boy listens to his great grandmother as she lies dying.

"… I've tasted every victual and danced every dance; now there's one last tart I haven't bit on, one tune I haven't whistled. But I'm not afraid. I'm truly curious. Death won't get a crumb by my mouth I won't taste and savor. So don't you worry over me. Now, all of you go, and let me find my sleep…."

Somewhere a door closed quietly…. A long time back, she thought, I dreamed a dream, and was enjoying it so much when someone wakened me, and that was the day when I was born. And now? Now, let me see…. She cast her mind back. Where was I? she thought. Ninety years … how to take up the … lost dream again? She put out a small hand. There … yes, that was it. She smiled. Deeper in the warm snow hill she turned her head upon her pillow. That was better … now she saw it shaping in her mind quietly…. Now she let the old dream touch and lift her from the snow….

"It's all right," whispered Great-grandma, as the dream floated her. "Like everything else in this life, it's fitting."

And the sea moved her back down the shore.

From *Dandelion Wine* by Ray Bradbury

To close your eyes
after realizing that
you have no control
over the opening
of your eyes is
a courageous
act of faith.

Making It Mine

Doug is the teenaged great-grandson of the woman who dies in the previous slice from the story. When his great-grandmother dies, the summer is ending. He's just lost his closest friend too. Childhood is behind him. Doug knows that nothing is going to be like it used to be. He pens in his journal, "You can't depend on things because … like tennis shoes, you can only run so far, so fast, and then the earth's got you again…. You can't depend on people because … they go away … your own folks can die…. So … if friends and near friends can go away for awhile or go away forever, or rust, or fall apart or die, and if people can be murdered, and if someone like Great-grandma, who was going to live forever, can die … if all of this is true … then I … someday … must…."

Doug never finishes the line. The fireflies in his mason jar stop giving him light. He pulls the covers over his head and sleeps with the inescapable truth of his own mortality.

Every one of us has the same moment. To close your eyes after realizing that you have no control over the opening of your eyes is a courageous act of faith. It takes the will of a hero and the heart of a child to rest peacefully after that bit of news really lands on your heart.

It happened for me when a friend was killed on the back of her boyfriend's motorcycle. They were sixteen or seventeen. A drunk driver never saw them. Her boyfriend died about four months later — but he had never regained consciousness. They were on their way to the beach. School was out. It was June.

I made up a bed on the pullout couch that night. Two friends were with me. One of the girls' boyfriends showed up about 1:00 A.M. We listened to music, watched TV, played cards, anything not to sleep. Someone made spaghetti about 6:00 A.M. I was in the kitchen when my brother, home on furlough from Vietnam, came downstairs and found us all half-awake, like zombies.

He ate spaghetti with us and told us jokes. Dad got up and started getting out stuff to fry bacon and green tomatoes. We decided to order daisies for the funeral. My brother convinced me to sing a Beatles' song with him. The line "She was just seventeen …" choked in my throat; I ran from the room straight into the arms of one of the other kids. We all clumped together and cried and rocked while my brother played his guitar and Dad fried bacon. The sounds of life going on were just right.

After a little while, we ate Dad's bacon and tomatoes with orange juice. My brother poured a tall glass and lifted it. He said nothing. We all lifted our glasses together. Not a word was said, but we all thought it, "To life and us and being seventeen…." A few minutes later we were all on the sofa bed asleep. I think Mom turned off the television and covered us with soft quilts when she woke up.

Dad's bacon, my brother's guitar, the tears and anguish, the comfort of Mom's quilt — these were the signs and sounds of life going on. Even faced with such tragedy as a young person's death, the sounds of life going on were just right and fitting.

Prayer Starter

The Lord is my shepherd, I shall not be in want.
   He makes me lie down in green pastures,
he leads me beside quiet waters,
   he restores my soul.
Even though I walk
   through the valley of the shadow of death,
I will fear no evil,
   for you are with me.

Psalm 23:1-3a, 4a

Jesus, you took the sting out of death. You remembered the dying man next to you even as you died. Remember me, remember the ones I love, and when we die, take us into your loving arms and give us peace.

Soul Writing

Write concerning your feelings about death — deaths that have taken family and friends, your own death. Have your feelings changed? Does your faith affect how you feel about death?

39
How Friendship Is Like a Fire

Something to Think About

The writer Henry Van Dyke muses about human beings and fire.

Friendship is one of life's most sacred gifts. Don't take your friends for granted. Build a friendship fire as a monument to the spirit and life of those you care about.

Humans are creatures who have made friends with the open fire. All the other creatures, in their natural state, are afraid of it. They look upon it with wonder and dismay. It fascinates them, at times, with its glittering eyes in the night…. But the attraction that masters them is one of dread, not of love. It is the witchcraft of the serpent's beguiling look…. Humans are the only creatures that dare to light a fire and live with it because they alone have learned how to put it out.

A fire in the woods is one thing — a comfort and a joy. Fire in the woods is another thing — a terror, uncontrollable fury, a burning shame.

[Van Dyke writes of a kind of fire — The Little Friendship Fire:] This form of fire does less work than any other in the world. Yet it is far from being useless; and I would be sorry to live without it. Its only use is to make a visible center of interest where there are two or three … or to supply a kind of companionship…. It is kindled and burns for no other purpose than to give you the sense of being at home and at ease. Why the fire should do this I cannot tell, but it does….

It is strange how long a small fire will leave its mark. The charred sticks, the black coals do not decay easily. If they lie well up the bank, out of reach of the spring floods, they will stay there for years. If you have chanced to build a rough fireplace of stones from the brook, it seems almost as if it would last forever.

Making It Mine

Scott Walker, author, wrote, "Vic Greene and I have been close friends since we were eleven years old…. There is something holy about sitting in silence by a fireside with a good and enduring friend…. Somehow the presence of someone bigger, someone ultimate, is felt…. And so, do such fireside moments come frequently? No, they don't. And are such friendships rare? Yes, they are, and worth their weight in gold…. Don't take your best friends for granted. Celebrate your history…. Their warm presence will cut the chill on many a winter night."

Friendship is like the friendship fire Van Dyke refers to. It might seem to have no useful purpose — but don't be fooled. Friendship will leave traces on interior regions all your life. You will be marked, for better or worse, by your friends. The best of friends provide their presence, a simple act of companionship, and we are ultimately and wonderfully changed by their loving, accepting, and enjoying us. We don't have to weigh our words with friends or be afraid of making slips. We can trust them to believe in us even when we've misunderstood their intentions.

Friendship is one of life's most sacred gifts. Don't take your friends for granted. Build a friendship fire as a monument to the spirit and life of those you care about. Let both of you warm away the cold by it.

 # Prayer Starter

A friend loves at all times,
   and kinsfolk are born to share adversity.
The purposes in the human mind are like deep water,
   but the intelligent will draw them out.
Many proclaim themselves loyal,
   but who can find one worthy of trust?

Proverbs 17:17; 20:5-6 (NRSV)

Jesus, I wish to be a good friend. You, who are Friend to all, teach me. Give me a sense of humor and laughter with my friends. Help us to be truthful with one another. Help us be gentle and strong together. Teach us to be more aware of you in one another and to treat with respect the bond that grows in our friendships.

Soul Writing

Write about what you like best in your closest friends. What friendships have lasted longest? Why? What qualities do you look for in your friends? What qualities do you have that draw friends to you?

40

The Queen of Attitude

Something to Think About

A young man changes as new ideas enter his head.

In each century since the beginning of the world, wonderful things have been discovered…. One of the new things people began to find out in the last century was that thoughts — just mere thoughts — are as powerful as electric batteries, as good for one as sunlight is, or as bad for one as poison.

To let a sad thought or a bad one get into your mind is as dangerous as letting a scarlet-fever germ get into your body. If you let it stay there after it has got in, you may never get over it as long as you live….

So long as Colin shut himself up in his room and thought only of his fears and weakness … he was a hysterical, half-crazy little hypochondriac, who knew nothing of the sunshine and spring, and also did not know that he could get well and could stand upon his feet if he tried….

When new, beautiful thoughts began to push out the old hideous ones, life began to come back to him…. Surprising things can happen to anyone who, when a disagreeable or discouraged thought comes into his mind, just has the sense to remember … and push it out by putting in an agreeable, determinedly courageous one. Two things cannot be in one place.

From *The Secret Garden* by Frances Hodgson Burnett

Don't let fear or ugly thoughts lodge in your head and take root. Exorcise the beasts from your mind as quickly as you can — make a habit of it.

Making It Mine

My daughter Andrea had nearly died in a car wreck. She was home after four weeks in the hospital. It was Christmas. Home. Safe. Surrounded by people who loved her.

And it seemed to me, she was also fragile. Very fragile. Andrea, however, didn't think herself fragile. Not from the moment she woke up in the Intensive Care Unit and pulled her respirator out so she could go home. The nurse told her that she couldn't walk on her broken legs. Andrea immediately swung her long legs around the edge of her bed and stood up. She nearly fell over, but not before standing for a second or two and startling all of us. You might say my daughter has, well, attitude.

She didn't want to stay in bed at Christmas. She wanted to be in the living room, near the tree, around the people; she wanted to play games and sing carols and listen to stories. Besides, friends from the youth group at church were planning to visit. She didn't want to be in bed. She wanted to put on jeans and makeup and put her hair in a braid and stick contacts in her eyes.

So she did. I watched with immense apprehension as the nurse helped her get ready that evening and my husband carried her into the living room. We propped her up on pillows just as the van pulled up and about twenty-five kids piled out. I panicked. I had expected a few young adults who would speak softly, give her balloons, and get out.

Twenty-five noisy kids crowded around her broken legs and fragile ribs. Twenty-five kids pressed close to hug her and tell her what was happening to mutual friends and give her cards and presents.... Twenty-five of them so filled our living room that I found myself in the kitchen helplessly watching them swarm around her.

And then I looked close. Andrea was glowing. Grinning. Laughing. Listening. Touching. Make no mistake about it — there was no way to miss the fact that she was recovering from a near-fatal accident — but something magical was happening.

Andrea, Queen of Attitude, wouldn't be treated like an invalid. And those remarkable, beautiful teenagers respected her enough not to treat her like one either. It was all in the attitude. Andrea knew that if she let my fears about her strength and frailty get inside her, she would never get it out. She wasn't going to adopt that view of herself.

They left no room for my maternal silliness and overprotection. Andrea's sense of herself left no room for that either. Two things cannot be in one place.

Don't let fear or ugly thoughts lodge in your head and take root. Exorcise the beasts from your mind as quickly as you can — make a habit of it. If you don't, they'll make a home with you. Instead, welcome only the noble, the good, the true, the beautiful in your mind. Remember, two things cannot be in one place.

Prayer Starter

Rejoice in the Lord always. I shall say it again: rejoice! Your kindness should be known to all. The Lord is near. Have no anxiety at all, but in everything, by prayer and petition, with thanksgiving, make your requests known to God. Then the peace of God ... will guard your hearts and minds in Christ Jesus.

Philippians 4:4-7 (NAB)

Holy Spirit, Giver of Life, my head is an empty bowl waiting to be filled. Fill it with good, healthy, nourishing things. Fill it with the gentle breath of God's love. Fill it with the fire of God's power. Fill it with thoughts of goodness and with determination to share that goodness with those I love.

Soul Writing

Think about your thoughts — not the Big Ideas you have, but the random, casual thoughts that come uninvited and stick around a while. How do these thoughts affect your moods, your work, your relationships? What control do you have over them? Should you have more control over them? Write about it.

41
A Fierce and Furious Love

Something to Think About

God's awesome
might isn't ever
used to crush us;
it's used to love us.
It walks us home. It
stays with us in the
night. It's just
out of sight.

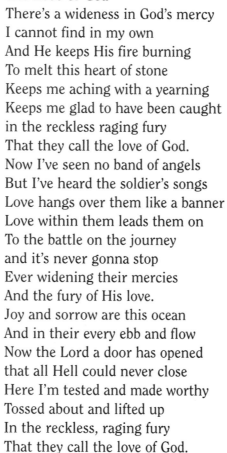

The Love of God
There's a wideness in God's mercy
I cannot find in my own
And He keeps His fire burning
To melt this heart of stone
Keeps me aching with a yearning
Keeps me glad to have been caught
in the reckless raging fury
That they call the love of God.
Now I've seen no band of angels
But I've heard the soldier's songs
Love hangs over them like a banner
Love within them leads them on
To the battle on the journey
and it's never gonna stop
Ever widening their mercies
And the fury of His love.
Joy and sorrow are this ocean
And in their every ebb and flow
Now the Lord a door has opened
that all Hell could never close
Here I'm tested and made worthy
Tossed about and lifted up
In the reckless, raging fury
That they call the love of God.

Written and recorded by the late Rich Mullins
(reproduction prohibited, used by permission)

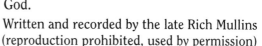

Making It Mine

Ever think of God's love as fierce? God's care for you as
tumultuous and wild?

There's a story in my family about my grandfather — a Native
American. He lived a very long life. No one knows how long because
they didn't keep track of the dates of births very well when he was

born. But when he died, about twenty years ago, he was guessed to be around a hundred years old.

We called him Pa. Pa lived in a tiny, dingy little cabin at the edge of a woods in Northern Michigan. Isolated — and that's how he liked it. His wife had died young, and he never remarried. He was father of twelve, grandfather of countless, great-grandfather of a new generation. He was a trapper. A woodsman. And he was a drunk. He drank the way asthmatics gulp for air. He drank in his isolation, and the isolation grew bigger each year as he alienated his children.

That, however, wasn't the Pa I knew. The Pa I knew danced me around a room, and told me stories, and taught me to name trees and plants and animals. He laughed often and loved hard.

I guess he ended up sort of like Puff the Magic Dragon, who loved a little boy who grew up and stopped coming around. I grew up and went away.

In his last years Pa used to walk every day to a bar about a mile from his cabin. He'd walk home again at night, after dark, in something close to a stupor. He was a legend in his neck of the woods. Old, upright, fierce-looking, tragic.

They say that usually on those long walks home in the deep of winter's darkest time you would see a shadow of something, or someone, walking just inside the wood's edge, step by step, with my grandfather until he was safely home. It wasn't a band of angels. It was said to be a bear. A very large black bear.

Many people reported seeing the old man and the bear day after day. When they buried my grandfather in an ancient cemetery in the woods, they say a bear watched from just inside the woods line. As the coffin was lowered, the bear rose to its hind legs and seemed to cry out from pain, then staggered off alone into the shadows of the woods. I don't know if it's true. But that's what they say.

And that's my own image of the love of God — the power and might and fierceness of a God who protects and watches over us. Fierce. You bet. But God's awesome might isn't ever used to crush us; it's used to love us. It walks us home. It stays with us in the night. It's just out of sight.

Prayer Starter

I lift up my eyes to the hills —
    where does my help come from?
My help comes from the Lord,
    the Maker of heaven and earth.
He will not let your foot slip —
    he who watches over you will not slumber;
the Lord will watch over your coming and going
    both now and forevermore.

Psalm 121:1-3, 8

Batter my heart ... for you as yet but knock! Breathe, shine, and seek to mend that I may rise and stand, overthrow me, and bend your force to break, blow, burn, and make me new.... Take me to you, imprison me, for I, except you enthrall me, never shall be free.

— *John Donne (adapted*)

Soul Writing

Write a story like the story they tell about Pa — a story that describes some aspect of the love of God for you.

42
Pursuing Dulcinea

Something to Think About

One of the greatest stories in the Spanish writer Cervantes's great novel, *Don Quixote*, concerns the relationship between Don Quixote and the woman Aldonza. God is like Don Quixote. We are Aldonza. God is Quixote who loves us relentlessly.

Aldonza is a waitress who serves drunken roughnecks during daylight. She takes care of them in other ways at night. Quixote, The Man of La Mancha, sees something else in this common hooker and barfly, something no one else has ever seen. He sees something Aldonza has certainly never seen in herself. Quixote sees a beauty of spirit and heart that has escaped the eyes of everyone else.

"My Lady," he calls her softly.

She looks at him, trying to hear the mockery, looking for the sneer and sees none. "Lady?"

"Yes, you are my Lady, and I will give you a new name. I will call you Dulcinea."

Later Aldonza-Dulcinea suffers one of the most hideous humiliations possible — she is raped. Don Quixote finds her. He had almost convinced her of her worth. The light was in her eyes; she would have believed in herself for the first time in her life, if not for this…. Quixote looks into her battered face. Her clothing is shredded; she is hysterical and beyond comfort.

"My Lady, Dulcinea, oh, my Lady, my Lady."

"Don't call me Lady," she cries. "Oh, God, don't call me a Lady. Can't you see me for what I am? I was born in a ditch by a mother who left me there naked and cold — too hungry to cry. I never blamed her. She left me there hoping I'd have the good sense to die. Don't call me Lady … I'm nothing at all."

She flees into the night from the man who loves her, while he calls after her, "But … you *are* my Lady."

The Man of La Mancha spends his life as a service to her, seeking the one he loves. To no avail. But, at the end, as he is dying from a broken heart, despised, misunderstood, and an outcast, a Spanish queen suddenly appears at his bedside.

Quietly, she kneels beside his bed and prays. He opens his weary, weak eyes and asks, "Who are you?"

Like Aldonza, we hardly ever see what we really are — beautiful, honorable Dulcineas. We don't even know how to dream the impossible for ourselves. God dreams the impossible dream.

"My Lord, don't you remember? You sang a song, don't you remember? 'To dream the impossible dream, to fight the unbeatable foe, to bear the unbearable sorrow, to run where the brave dare not go….' My Lord, don't you remember? You gave me a new name, you called me Dulcinea." She stands with the bearing of a queen and says, "I am your Lady."

Making It Mine

Like Aldonza, we hardly ever see what we really are — beautiful, honorable Dulcineas. We don't even know how to dream the impossible for ourselves. God dreams the impossible dream for us when we're unable to pick ourselves up one more time. God fights the unbeatable foe when our arms are broken. God bears the unbearable sorrow with us, carrying the full weight of it.

The only way to understand, even remotely, what it costs God to love us is to consider and ponder the crucifixion of Christ. This is the story for all who try to love when love isn't easy and it's a reminder that when we do so, God is united with us in the high price we pay to genuinely love.

Singer Michael Card once sang, "… all who would seek to love — a thorn is all the world has to give." God isn't hesitant about loving us despite the cost. God is like Don Quixote.

Prayer Starter

Give thanks to the Lord, for he is good;
   his love endures forever.
He turned the desert into pools of water
   and the parched ground into flowing springs;
there he brought the hungry to live,
   and they founded a city where they could settle.

Psalm 107:1, 35-36

God, I often can't see the beauty in me. The deepest truths about me are truths you have to reveal to me. Show me — somehow — this holy vision of myself. Help me see myself as you see me.

 # Soul Writing

Write about the good qualities that others have noticed in you. If God were to write a letter to you describing how he sees you, what would it say? Write that letter.

43
Forgiveness: Free at Last

Something to Think About

The writer Ken Gire remembers a kid he hurt a long time ago.

I was eight, I think, maybe nine. A friend and I were playing catch, and a kid named Reese from around the block wanted to horn in on our game…. We pushed him and hit him, and by the time it was all over we had split his lip and broken one of his permanent teeth. As he ran home crying, my friend and I laughed and congratulated ourselves with "That'll-teach-him" kind of talk.

A few minutes later his sister came running around the corner. She was older than we were and bigger, and as angry as she was she could have beaten up the both of us. She didn't. But through her tears she yelled at us and told us off and made me feel the way I should have felt all along — ashamed.

I was not a bad boy. The boy I was playing catch with was not a bad boy. But together we did something terribly bad that to this day I terribly regret…. Not long after that, Reese moved. His father was in the Air Force so I suspect he moved a lot over the years, and I suspect it was always difficult being the new kid on the block…. As for me … I have moved a total of ten times…. Few things have survived those ten moves and almost nothing from my old neighborhood.

Except this. A letter from Reese …
I beat him up.
"Dear Kenny."
I broke one of his permanent teeth.
"I hope you're OK."
And I laughed about it.
"Sincerely, Reese."
… Between the lines in Reese's letter, there was forgiveness … forgiveness I desperately needed. I didn't know it then. I do now.

From *Windows of the Soul* by Ken Gire

Ultimately, every violation against God, love, others, weighs us down and we carry the collection around. It must be cut off. That's what the Sacrament of Reconciliation is about.

Making It Mine

Ashley Cleveland, musician and songwriter, wrote about saying good-bye to our pasts and all that means in a song titled "At the End of a Long Good-bye." She writes, "This is where my future lies, at the end of a long good-bye…. Hope becomes my sweet surprise."

It takes a long time to say good-bye to the mistakes and bad things we do. It's not that we aren't trying to be better people. We're trying. It just takes a while sometimes. What we need is what Ken Gire got from Reese — someone to forgive us.

I saw a movie about a mercenary brute who has lived a horrendous life of violence, most of it aimed at the natives of the land he's in. The man has a conversion and deeply regrets what he's done. He decides to give himself a penance; he carries a heavy pack on his back filled with weight that makes his every move difficult. He carries it night and day for a very long time.

One day, one of the people he has violated, a native, walks up to him and cuts the pack off. No one else could have freed him except the one violated. The act of forgiveness gives the mercenary-turned-Christian the new start he craved.

Ultimately, every violation against God, love, others, weighs us down and we carry the collection around. It must be cut off. That's what the Sacrament of Reconciliation is about. It's a wonderful chance Catholics have: God's gift of new starts.

A friend of mine has painted a portrait of a little girl who is walking away. Her head is up, her pigtails swinging, her shoulders straight as she strides off. She is obviously walking away and proud of it. That's what the Sacrament of Reconciliation allows us to do. Walk away without the pack on our back. Walk away to start over again.

Prayer Starter

Have mercy on me, O God,
    according to your unfailing love;
according to your great compassion
    blot out my transgressions.
Cleanse me … and I will be clean;
    wash me, and I will be whiter than snow.
Create in me a pure heart, O God,
    and renew a steadfast spirit within me.

Psalms 51:1, 7, 10

Lord of my darkest place: Let in your light.
Lord of my greatest fear: Let in your peace.
Lord of my most bitter shame: Let in your word of grace.
Lord of my oldest grudge: Let in your forgiveness.
— Allison Pepper

Soul Writing

Write about forgiveness. What do you need to be forgiven for? Is someone looking for forgiveness from you? How did you feel after the last time you went to the Sacrament of Reconciliation?

44
No One's Perfect

Something to Think About

I was old enough to think I knew how to drive but young enough not to be able to drive…. I happily volunteered to wash the family car. The whole point, of course, was to be able to drive it: the car was never quite in the right place in relation to the hose, and so I drove it back and forth over about fifteen feet of driveway.

I had the unhappy fortune one day to have backed over the bucket just as my father came out of the house. Neither of us can remember what was on his mind … something [had] filled and troubled his mind when he shot through the back door … a Man with a Mission.

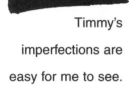

Timmy's imperfections are easy for me to see. My own are not. I annoy people. I have odd habits. I make mistakes. I expect others to overlook my imperfections.

A squashed bucket under the axle he didn't need. I hadn't hurt the car. The bucket was only bent. No big deal, or so I thought. But Dad erupted in uncharacteristic anger.

"Dumb kid! Why don't you watch what you're doing? Give me the keys!"

And then he jumped in the driver's seat, started the engine, threw it into reverse, and backed out of the driveway … right into the neighbor's car.

I did not laugh. I wanted to. Never in my life had I wanted to laugh more … not during church when Danny farted during the pastoral prayer, not when Cousin Bob drove the pickup through the wall of Uncle Harold's barn, not when we tied Aunt Pearl's underwear in knots — never had I so wanted to laugh. I might have been careless with buckets, but I wasn't stupid.

When I finally had the courage to mention the incident twenty years later, we both had a good laugh. Now he's the first to admit the obvious; had he known he was about to smash into the neighbor's Chevy, he wouldn't have been so upset that I ran over a bucket.

From *Finding Happiness in the Most Unlikely Places*
by Donald McCullough

Making It Mine

My friend Timmy is twenty-six years old now. When we first met he was eighteen, and drooling on my computer — literally. Timmy is brilliant. Genuine genius material who works with computers like most of us work with simple arithmetic. Timmy wasn't easy to take though. His quite evident, and rather distracting, speech impediment, added to a very eccentric personality, meant that when he arrived to work on my computer I usually tried to avoid conversations with him.

But Timmy liked me. He looked forward to talking with me. One day I couldn't get out of the way soon enough and found myself face to face in a discussion on microchips and theology with him. Lucky for me, his braces had come off and he wasn't drooling anymore. I felt like a pretty big person putting up with him that day. During the course of our discussion I misquoted an author we both like. Timmy didn't point out my mistake. He smiled at me wide and said, "I knew what you meant — no one's ever perfect. You're nice, that's what matters most."

Timmy's imperfections are easy for me to see. My own are not. I annoy people. I have odd habits. I make mistakes. I expect others to overlook my imperfections. I even take it for granted. Jesus called it choking on a flea while swallowing a camel or seeing the sliver in someone's eye when your own has a log in it.

Crushed buckets happen. But we can get so wrapped up in the little things that we smash up big-time. No one's perfect.

"Always we begin again," Saint Benedict wrote. Let's do the same.

 # Prayer Starter

The Lord knows the thoughts of man;
   he knows that they are futile.
Judgment will again be founded on righteousness,
   and all the upright in heart will follow it.

Psalm 94:11, 15

Lord, save me from getting stuck on the simple failures of those around me; help me overlook the shortcomings of others. We are all prone to smash buckets every now and then. When I search for faults and blame, let me look inside myself first, always consider my contribution, and have the courage not to shift blame.

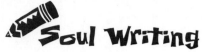 **Soul Writing**

Write about a time or times when others seemed to focus on your mistakes rather than their own. How did you feel? When have you done the same?

45
Don't Try to Steer When You're Confused

Something to Think About

An inexperienced sailor starts to panic in a thick fog.

From the impenetrable core of the mist I heard the captain's voice coming at me clear as a warning horn, repeating something he had told me during one of my early sailing lessons, when I pushed the tiller the wrong way and almost threw the boat into a dangerous jibe.

"Let go of the tiller!" he was saying. "Just let go of the tiller! Don't try to steer when you're confused!"

I followed his advice and the blue sloop did exactly what she was supposed to do.... I went up on the bow and tossed the anchor overboard and sat on the foredeck, waiting for a revelation, a glimmer of light, to tell me where I was and which way I had to go.... What I had to do was sit calmly on the deck and empty my mind of all its preconceived notions and prejudices about the nature of fog, and then I would be able to detect the one constant in the swirling mist that would set me on my rightful course.

Calm yourself. Pray. Don't try to steer when you're confused.

From *First You Have to Row a Little Boat: Reflections on Life and Living*
by Richard Bode

Making It Mine

When you're confused, don't try to steer. Good advice on life from a sailor. Don't make decisions; don't set out in a new direction when you can't see where you're going. The fog was thick. He had to get his bearings, remember where he was, find a clue for how to get home.

He needed to locate the "one constant in the swirling mist that would set me on my rightful course." He had to get a fix on something stable and constant. Eventually he remembered that a boat is like a weather vane: it always points into the wind — an east wind.

Going to the foredeck, quieting himself, anchoring — these were acts of prayer. Emptying himself of fears and prejudices — also prayer. It was a quieting down so he could fix again on one thing that couldn't be lost in the fog. It was obvious and simple — but in the confusion he didn't remember the obvious.

We've all been in the same spot as this sailor, haven't we? No matter what decisions you face or how confused life gets, you too have constants that can give you direction. Family. Church. Faith. Self-respect. God.

A children's toy that always reminds me of this is a hard, clear plastic ball. Inside is a center bar with a mouse holding on to it. Because the mouse holds on to the bar he stays upright even as the ball rolls and tumbles.

The secret is in holding on to the Center. You'll tumble a bit, but you'll always be standing up.

Bode, our sailor, tells another story — this one about how he lost a rudder. His friend and mentor Oscar built another one for him. Without a solid, strong rudder, steering is impossible. Writes Bode: "What I remember most is that one day long ago I lost my rudder, and then a superb craftsman gave it back to me, and ever since I've been at great pains not to lose it again."

Everyone gets lost sometimes. We don't always know how to make choices. Just remember that certain rudders have been crafted by God for the purpose of giving you stability and direction. Hold on to these. Calm yourself. Pray. Don't try to steer when you're confused.

 ## Prayer Starter

Turn my eyes away from worthless things;
    preserve my life according to your word.
I have sought your face with all my heart;
    be gracious to me according to your promise.
I have considered my ways
    and have turned my steps to your statutes.

Psalm 119:37, 58-59

In the words of St. Patrick I pray, "May the strength of God pilot us; may the power of God preserve us; may the wisdom of God instruct us.... May the way of God direct us...."

Soul Writing

What is the center or unchanging realities that you hold on to for stability and direction? Write about them. Describe them. Have you ever made a decision when you did not have a grip on these realities? What was the result?

46
The Work of Human Hands

Something to Think About

Watching killer whales, the Christian novelist Frederick Buechner experiences a moment of grace.

Several winters ago my wife and I and our then twenty-year-old daughter, Sharmy, went to that great tourist extravaganza near Orlando, Florida, called Sea World. There is a lot of hoopla to it — crowds of people, loud music, Mickey Mouse T-shirts, and so on, but the main attraction makes it all worthwhile … the bleachers where we sat were packed.

The way the show began was that at a given signal they released into the tank five or six killer whales, as we call them … and no creatures under heaven could have looked less killerlike as they went racing around and around in circles. What with the dazzle of sky and sun, the beautiful young people on the platform, the soft southern air … it was as if the whole creation — men and women and beasts and sun and water and earth and sky and, for all I know, God himself — was caught up in one great, jubilant dance of unimaginable beauty. And then, right in the midst of it, I was astonished to find that my eyes were filled with tears.

When the show was over and I turned to my wife and daughter beside me to tell them what had happened … there had been tears in their eyes also.

From *The Longing for Home: Recollections and Reflections*
by Frederick Buechner

Something holy and shocking takes place. God isn't just imaged or reflected. God does one better. God shows up. God is incarnate in the work of human hands.

Making It Mine

At Valparaiso University in Valparaiso, Indiana, there is a magnificent chapel called the Chapel of the Resurrection. It doesn't look like much from the outside, just another piece of modern architecture built in the 1950s. Go inside.

I've been there three times, and it always chokes me up. Stand in the center aisle and slowly walk toward the towering stained glass and the altar area where a crucifix with a resurrected Christ embracing all of creation shoots up out of the floor like a geyser. The stained glass is stunning. The crucifix magnificent.

But that's not what chokes me up. I've seen modern architecture before.

As you walk toward the front of the chapel something magical happens; the walls of the chapel seem to expand and draw you into the Christ and the colors and light. It is a completely unexpected effect. It's all in the design of the building. Even though I've seen it, it has caught me off guard each time. It leaves you breathless and it leaves you worshiping.

That's what a chapel should do.

Author Frederick Buechner and his family experienced the same thing at Sea World. Think about it — Sea World. Tourist trap extraordinaire. What Sea World has in common with Valparaiso's devastatingly beautiful chapel is that both are the products of human labor. And in the human labor, something holy and shocking takes place. God isn't just imaged or reflected. God does one better. God shows up. God is incarnate in the work of human hands.

There's magic in your hands. Hear it again, children of God. There's magic in those hands of yours. We are created to create. Gifted to gift. Made to make. The next time you hear someone fussing about how something is only "man-made," stop and think again. That's a pretty remarkable thing they're saying. Here we are — creatures. We didn't come into being by any effort of our own, and yet we go about bringing into being all sorts of wonder and beauty and goodness with our hands. The work of our hands is holy.

We offer it in Eucharist as we pray with the priest, "… the work of human hands" and lift the cup. God is still creating our world and our universe. We're in with him in the stuff of creation as we use our hands to build. Don Henley — drummer, songwriter, and former Eagle — was just repeating the words of the Bible when he sang, "… So, whatever your hands find to do, you must do with all your heart…."

 # Prayer Starter

May the favor of the Lord our God rest upon us;
  establish the work of our hands for us —
  yes, establish the work of our hands.

Psalm 90:17

Lord, let my life be a space for you to work in the world.
Clean away the junk in my spirit and mind.
Make my heart bigger.
Give strength to my hands,
so that all I do
is the work of your love in my life.

Soul Writing

Jot down the ideas that come to mind when you think of "work." What's the purpose of work? What place does it have in life other than to earn a living? Write about a time you have experienced work as a cooperative effort with God.

47
Cleaning Up — Inside and Out

Something to Think About

My friend's daughter, Patty, nineteen, was in her room — cleaning. My friend announced this as if it were a day to remember. It was.

Patty had dated the same boy since she was sixteen. He wasn't good for Patty. In the last months it had gotten worse. He told her how to dress. He questioned where she went and with whom. He called her in the middle of the night just to be sure she was home. He had hit her once that her mother knew of.

The day before the cleaning spree, Patty had told the boy she wasn't going to see him anymore.

Patty wasn't just cleaning her room, she was imposing order on chaos. She was taking her life back. She was creating a new universe from the chaos of the old one.

What was happening inside of her had to be expressed on the outside; that's how powerful the change was and how powerfully it impacted her whole world. Before she had finished, Patty had even repainted her bedroom, bought new drapes, and stuffed all evidence of this young man into a box and buried it in the family attic.

Here's the secret — don't wait until the chaos clears before you start putting things in order.

Making It Mine

When my children were teenagers, I could tell what was happening on the inside by how things looked on the outside. Especially how their rooms looked. When they felt good about themselves and in control, the room would be orderly. When chaos reigned inside, it reigned outside.

Who we are on the inside is revealed on the outside in obvious ways. I once watched a little boy, just a year old, take all his toy trucks and line them up straight and orderly across the living room. The son of an accountant — it's in his genes.

We all have days when it seems that chaos rules. When this happens, try using this basic inside-equals-outside principle in your favor. Here's the secret — don't wait until the chaos clears before you start putting things in order. Act as if things are in order. Do something that counters how you feel. If you don't *feel* loving toward your friend — *act* loving. If you feel messed up inside — clean your car. If you don't want to talk to anyone — take a walk, go to the library, visit an elderly relative. Challenge the havoc inside.

Something surprising happens. The peacefulness, calmness, or generosity we're craving inside starts to appear when we act as if it were already there. I know it sounds impossible. Try it.

The reverse of what I've said is also true. Your surroundings affect your feelings. A messy room feeds a messy heart. These two feed on each other. All you have to do is break the cycle somewhere, take charge, and things happen.

Jesus did this when he told crippled people to walk and blind people to see. He called reality into being. Okay, that's a little different, but the principle works the same. You are not a helpless bystander in the bedlam. Order it. Shape it. Line up your blocks. Pack away the old. Paint up the new. It is a very good kind — or, to put it another way, "God-kind" — of thing to do to bring order out of chaos.

 ## Prayer Starter

Though an army besiege me,
   my heart will not fear;
though war break out against me,
   even then will I be confident.
Wait for the Lord;
   be strong and take heart
   and wait for the Lord.

Psalm 27:3, 14

God, only if you stay at the center of my soul will the chaos ever be ordered. I'll have peace only if you are present in all that I do. When I want to give in, hold me. When I want to run, stop me. When I want to lash out and hurt others, restrain me. Keep me with you.

 **Soul Writing**

Write about a time when it seemed that chaos was ruling in your life. What happened that resolved your feelings? How do the exterior and interior affect each other? What might you do now to take a first step in resolving some chaos you're experiencing?

48
How to Be Tall
(No Matter What Your Height)

Something to Think About

S. D. Gaede reflects on his desire to be as tall as his father, well over six feet.

During my senior year in high school, I must have looked at myself in the mirror three times a day, just to see whether I was tall yet.... I certainly wanted to be tall. Every time I went up for a layup, or tried an overhead smash, or looked at Cheryl Tiegs....

Me, thirteen years old and sitting in the driver's seat of Dad's pickup, barely able to look over the steering wheel but driving right through the middle of town, nevertheless. Why this abuse of California traffic regulations?

Because Dad is sitting in the back of the pickup, delivering one-hundred-pound bags of potatoes to an assortment of friends, relatives, and needy citizens. Even for a legalist, some things are more important than law. And so, three years before I was qualified for a license, I was meandering around the streets of town in my Dad's pickup, while he ran back and forth — from pickup to house and back again — toting those hundred-pound bags on his shoulders, and delivering the fruit of his labor to those he loved.

... I didn't mind being smaller than Dad. The bags were heavy, for one thing.... But there was something else, as well.... It seemed embarrassing to me. Below my dignity, not to mention my social standing.... Why didn't he pay someone else to deliver them? Why did he have to take the time and energy to cart these crazy potatoes around town himself?

I was smaller than my Dad.... Dad on the other hand, was tall ... and yet, he had no difficulty whatsoever putting others above himself. It was easy for him to be small, in other words. And I think that's why God made him tall. Very, very tall.

... My Dad kept at it ... delivering potatoes. Entrusting me with responsibilities (like driving a pickup) long before I deserved to be trusted. Letting me tag along with him, even though he knew I would get in the way. Just being tall. Very, very tall.

From Surprised by God by S. D. Gaede

Mary has saved the life of a local man. He lived in a burned-out shell of a house that was overgrown with weeds and lacked heat and water. That's just not acceptable to Mary; so she did something about it.

Making It Mine

The story above isn't about height. It's about people who have power, advantaged people who don't take advantage of their advantage and don't need to make a name for themselves. Remarkable people.

I know a few like that. Mary, for example. Mary is Father Dan's partner in retreat ministry and close friend of many years, longer than most of you have been alive. Mary is short, maybe five feet tall. I'm not tall either, but she's even shorter than I am. I've known short people who seem intent on making others feel small — just so they can feel big. Not Mary. I spend an hour with Mary and I feel six feet tall.

Mary has saved the life of a local man. He lived in a burned-out shell of a house that was overgrown with weeds and lacked heat and water. That's just not acceptable to Mary; so she did something about it. During Project People (see Sessions 27 and 28) she organized a crew headed by Father Dan to clean and fix up the man's place. They cleared the jungle away from his house and helped him out of isolation.

A while later, when the man was very sick, on the edge of death, one of the neighbors called Mary — these were neighbors who would not have gotten near what they considered to be a crazy old hermit (if they even knew he existed) a few months earlier.

Mary went to the hospital with him. She worked things out so that he now has a brand-new house, with water and electricity and heat. Note this — she has other things to do with her life. For Mary, there's no shortage of family and friends and work and all the good things we value. She's advantaged that way. Yet, she's so unaware of herself that she wouldn't consider anything she does remarkable. Mary goes through life being very tall.

 # Prayer Starter

"You know that the rulers ... lord it over them, and the great ones make their authority over them felt. But it shall not be so among you. Rather, whoever wishes to be great among you shall be your servant; ... Just [as] ... the Son of Man did not come to be served but to serve...."

Matthew 20:25-26, 28 (NAB)

*Suffer us, O Lord, never to think
that we have knowledge enough to need no teaching,
wisdom enough to need no correction,
talents enough to need no grace,
goodness enough to need no progress,
humility enough to need no repentance,
devotion enough to need no quickening,
strength sufficient without your Spirit;
lest standing ... we fall back forever.*
— *Eric Milner-White*

Soul Writing

Write about a person like Mary you have known who is "tall" enough to put others first. Reflect on the ideal of leadership such servants convey. What qualities of leadership do you respond to? How can you cultivate them in yourself?

49
A Big, Brave Man

Something to Think About

His name was Larry-John. I didn't know him very well, but I'll never forget him. I was in junior high. Larry-John was older, centuries older. He was in high school, probably seventeen, maybe eighteen.

Her name was … I can't remember her name, as hard as I've tried. She was the object of everyone's jokes. She lived three blocks from me, but she walked home alone. She was always nice to me. Really nice. She would tell me how great I looked. She would be excited when I scored at the top of my class. She once commented (in high school), "When I see how nice the boys are that you date, I figure you must be someone special." Her sincerity was heartbreaking.

We're at a football game. I'm with my older brother, who is a senior and seems to haul me all over the place with him. Larry-John is his friend and I've just met him for the very first time. He kisses my hand. He's six feet four, has black hair, dark blue eyes, square jaw. Superman had nothing on him for muscles. I'm in love and sitting between the big brother I adore and the man I plan to marry. Life is perfect.

He wasn't someone you would think of as a hero. He was an ordinary skinny seventeen-year-old boy with braces.

Two rows below us sits the girl everyone ignores. Larry-John isn't from our school. He didn't know how it was with her. At halftime some of the boys from our class start taunting the girl. It gets ugly. She's in tears, and her hands are over her ears. I lean back behind my brother so I don't have to see it when they finish her off.

Suddenly Larry-John leaves my side to go to the girl. He looked like he would hit someone. But he didn't. He informed my male classmates that they were low-life, scum of the earth, not worthy to share the planet with the object of their scorn.

He takes the girl's hand and before I know it, she is sitting between me and Larry-John, where she stays for the entire game. He asks her to join us for burgers afterward, but she lets him off the hook; her mother is picking her up. "Gee," he lies, "you look old enough to drive." She floated to her mother's car.

I'm ashamed to admit that I didn't have a flood of conscience and begin treating the girl better. She never became my best friend. We did walk home together once in a while after that. She sat with me at lunch sometimes. What she wrote in my yearbook would have made you think I was her closest friend in all the world. But I knew better. I gave her crumbs. Larry-John had given her one night of being the princess, one night of protection in the long string of nights standing alone against the cruelty of being on the outside. I remember Larry-John because he was a hero.

Making It Mine

Heroic acts are more common than we think. Most of us would put ourselves in the way of the danger when something or someone we care about is threatened. When I was a senior in high school, a boy who had cared about me for a long time put himself between me and a car I didn't see. Fortunately, neither of us was hurt. He wasn't someone you would think of as a hero. He was an ordinary skinny seventeen-year-old boy with braces.

For some people, like the girl in the story, it's heroic to keep getting up every morning. To just keeping showing up at school, at games, at dances — that was more heroic than I ever understood back then. It's heroic sometimes just to be honest. When another friend got caught having a party at her parents' cottage and was grounded the rest of the summer, she showed up at youth group the same weekend. She didn't try to blame anyone but herself. She'd messed up, but she was hero enough to face it.

You know stories like these. Your friends. You. We all have hero potential. As another musician put it, "… there's got to be some hero in me." There is, just like Larry-John.

Prayer Starter

In my integrity you uphold me
> and set me in your presence forever.
>> Psalm 41:12

Father, you make me stronger than I know, braver than I've ever understood. I want your approval more than the approval of others. I want to be strong in opposing what is unjust and tender toward what is broken. Give me this strength and tenderness. This is my prayer.

 Soul Writing

Write about courage. Think about instances of "quiet courage" you have seen — the bravery of a Larry-John; the resolve of an unpopular classmate who keeps showing up every day. What is the bravest action you have ever seen? What is the bravest thing you have ever done?

50
Push Back the Darkness

Something to Think About

Nathaniel Hawthorne's classic novel The Scarlet Letter *tells the story of Hester Prynne, convicted of adultery in pre-Revolutionary Puritan New England and forced to wear a scarlet-colored "A" for the rest of her life as a constant reminder of her sin. Hester behaves courageously. She leaves the dismal little town but eventually returns. The scarlet letter, the symbol of her alienation and brokenness, eventually is transformed.*

Keep dreaming the wild dreams of justice and freedom they tell us. But it's not enough. Walk into your world forgiving and loving and setting things right.

Of her own free will, for not the sternest magistrate of that iron period would have imposed it — [Hester] resumed the symbol [the scarlet "A"] of which we have related so dark a tale. Never afterwards did it quit her bosom. But in the lapse of toilsome, thoughtful, and self-devoted years that made up Hester's life, the scarlet letter ceased to be a stigma which attracted the world's scorn and bitterness, and became a type of something to be sorrowed over, and looked upon with awe…. Women, more especially — in the continually recurring trials of wounded, wasted, wronged, misplaced or erring passion — or with the dreary burden of a heart unyielded — came to Hester's cottage, demanding why they were so wretched, and what the remedy!

Hester comforted and counseled them, as best she might. She assured them too, of her firm belief, that at some brighter period, when the world should have grown ripe for it, in Heaven's own time, a new truth would be revealed.

From *The Scarlet Letter* by Nathaniel Hawthorne

Making It Mine

The popular musical production *Joseph and His Amazing Technicolor Dreamcoat* tells the biblical story of Joseph, a young man, his father's favorite, who dreams wildly and holds court to visions. To tell the world how much he loves Joseph, his father gives him a coat of many colors. An amazing coat. It is splendid beyond description.

Hester Prynne wears a badge of shame; Joseph wears a badge of honor. Both Hester and Joseph wear their identity for all the world to see. Shamed, exalted — right out there in the open.

Both learn that who we are isn't at all determined by who others say we are. Hard times hit them both. Hester is scorned. Joseph is sold into slavery by his jealous brothers and ends up in prison. They lose it all. The favored one and the punished one end up looking quite a lot alike.

Both learn in the depths of their despair that they must hold on to the truth about who they are, hold tight to their dreams, and believe in the deepest true self they know. They both discover that it only happens when they live by faith and when they forgive those who have mistreated them.

The favored ones and the persecuted ones end up making the same choices. We end up learning the same lessons. We end up more alike than different. Who would think it — Hester and Joseph?

In prison Joseph sings a haunting song from behind the bars and we sense he's coming to himself for the first time.

"Close every door to me, lock me away, keep those I love from me … if my life were important I would ask will I live or die, but I know the answers lie far from this place … for the children of Israel are never alone…."

Joseph and Hester each come to realize that the world they dream of is still coming to be. They are both prophets and visionaries who dream of a world being born — and somewhere along the way they begin to act on their dreams. By forgiving his brothers Joseph pushes back the darkness that almost swallowed him up; by returning and opening her home to those who had ridiculed and scorned her, Hester pushes back the darkness.

Keep dreaming the wild dreams of justice and freedom they tell us. But it's not enough. Walk into your world forgiving and loving and setting things right. The world grows ripe and a new truth comes. This is the Gospel of our Lord.

Prayer Starter

Part your heavens, O Lord, and come down;
  touch the mountains, so that they smoke.
Send forth lightning and scatter (the enemies);
  shoot your arrows and rout them.
I will sing a new song to you, O God.

Psalm 144:5-6, 9a

God, teach me to build my dreams on you. Though you won't hold back all the storms, when they hit I will be safe. Into our battered world keep your kingdom coming among us. Make my dreams true, my heart faithful, my eyes clear. When all else crumbles, let me hold on to you. And I will never be alone.

 **Soul Writing**

As you consider building a future, what dreams are most important to you? In what ways do others determine who you are? How might your dreams tell you something about who you really are?

Theme Index

Note: The entries in this index are cited by session (chapter) numbers, not page numbers.

Our Sunday Visitor...
Your Source for Discovering the Riches of the Catholic Faith

Our Sunday Visitor has an extensive line of materials for young children, teens, and adults. Our books, Bibles, booklets, CD-ROMs, audios, and videos are available in bookstores worldwide.

To receive a FREE full-line catalog or for more information, call **Our Sunday Visitor** at **1-800-348-2440**. Or write, **Our Sunday Visitor** / 200 Noll Plaza / Huntington, IN 46750.

Please send me:__ A catalog
Please send me materials on:
  __ Apologetics and catechetics   __ Reference works
  __ Prayer books   __ Heritage and the saints
  __ The family   __ The parish

Name_____

Address_____Apt._____

City_____State ____Zip_____

Telephone (   ) _____

A73BBABP

Please send a friend:__ A catalog
Please send a friend materials on:
  __ Apologetics and catechetics   __ Reference works
  __ Prayer books   __ Heritage and the saints
  __ The family   __ The parish

Name_____

Address_____Apt._____

City_____State ____Zip_____

Telephone (   ) _____

A73BBABP

Our Sunday Visitor
200 Noll Plaza
Huntington, IN 46750
1-800-348-2440
OSVSALES@AOL.COM

Your Source for Discovering the Riches of the Catholic Faith